To

~~xxxxxxxxxx~~ and ~~xxxxxxxx~~

Read This at your leisure.
It's a pleasure.

and   בא צאר

~~xxxxxxxxxx~~

Pesach - Nisan 5768

ALSO BY NATALIE d'ARBELOFF

Creating in Collage

An Artist's Workbook

Designing With Natural Forms

Augustine's True Confession

The Augustine Adventures

The Joy of Letting Women Down

and many limited edition handmade artists books,

some of which are shown at

www.nataliedarbeloff.com/books.html

the God Interviews

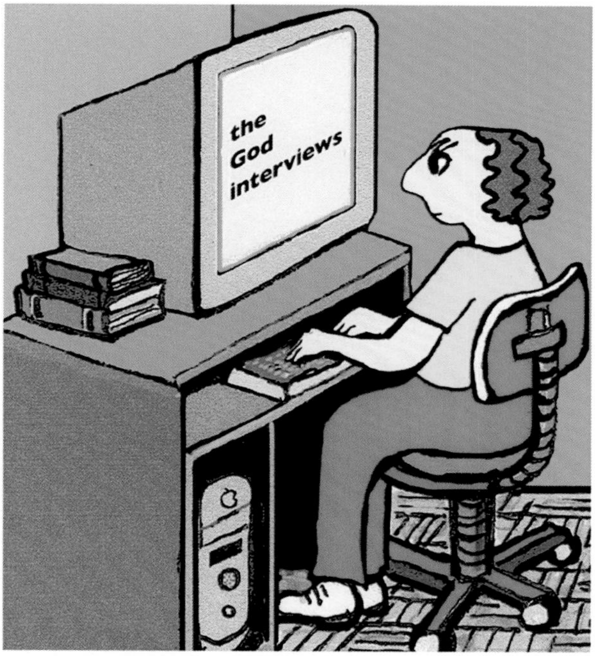
the
God
interviews

First published in 2006 by
NdA Press
endapress@blueyonder.co.uk

ISBN-10: 0-906487-13-7
ISBN-13: 978-0-906487-13-6
EAN: 9780906487136

the God Interviews

Natalie d'Arbeloff

NdA Press

For my family and my friends

Why do you need a foreword?

 To help potential readers make up their minds as to whether this book is their kind of thing or not.

 They can see that by looking at the cover.

 But they won't know what my position is regarding...um...you.

 Your position?

 Well, people who think religion is the opiate of the people might be put off by a book called the God Interviews and those who are believers might think I'm joking.

 That's always misquoted. What he actually said was: religion is the sigh of the oppressed creature, the heart of a heartless world, and the soul of soulless conditions. It is the opium of the people.

 Whatever.

 No, not whatever. Karl Marx, 1843. Great stuff, if a bit verbose.

 You agree with him?

 Lovely beard. Looked and sounded like me in Old Testament role.

 Please! I don't want people to think this book preaches, promotes, attacks, defends or satirises any religion.

 Allright then, what is this book?

 It's...um...deep...but not heavy.....dialogues between two cartoon characters who are actual representations of the real me and the real you.

 What is your position on reality?

 I think we've got a foreword.

ONE

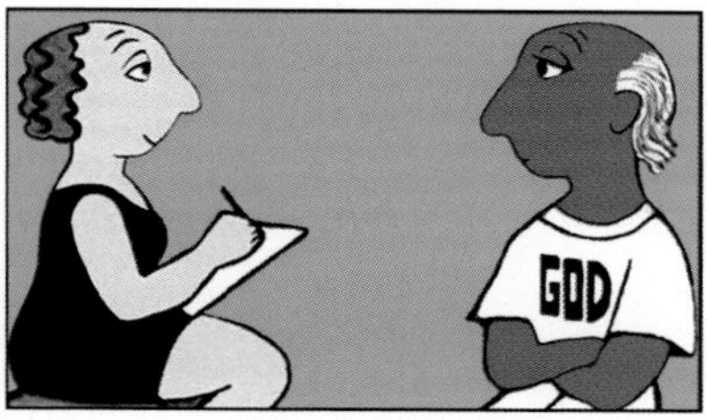
GOD

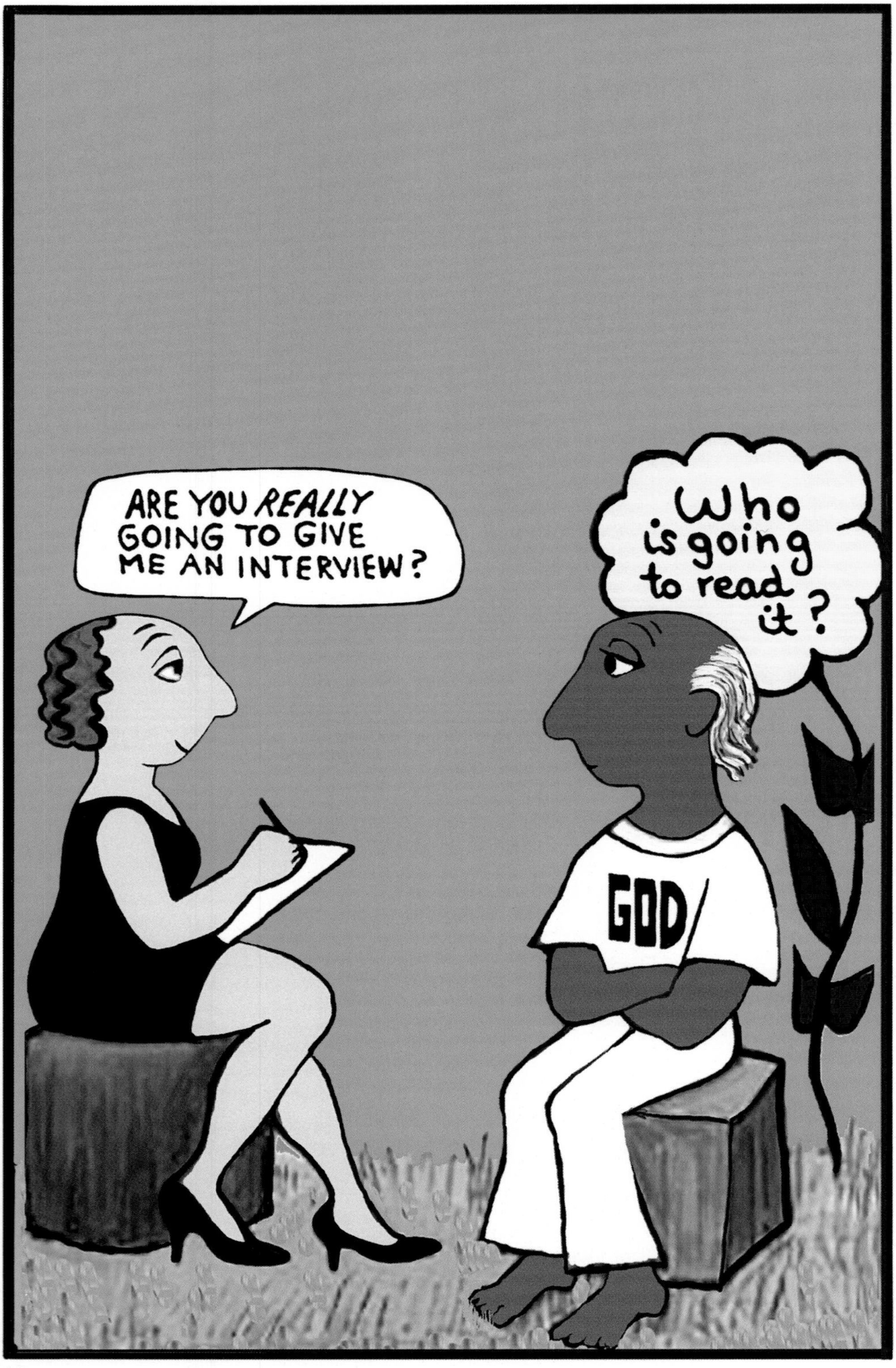
ARE YOU *REALLY* GOING TO GIVE ME AN INTERVIEW?
Who is going to read it?
GOD

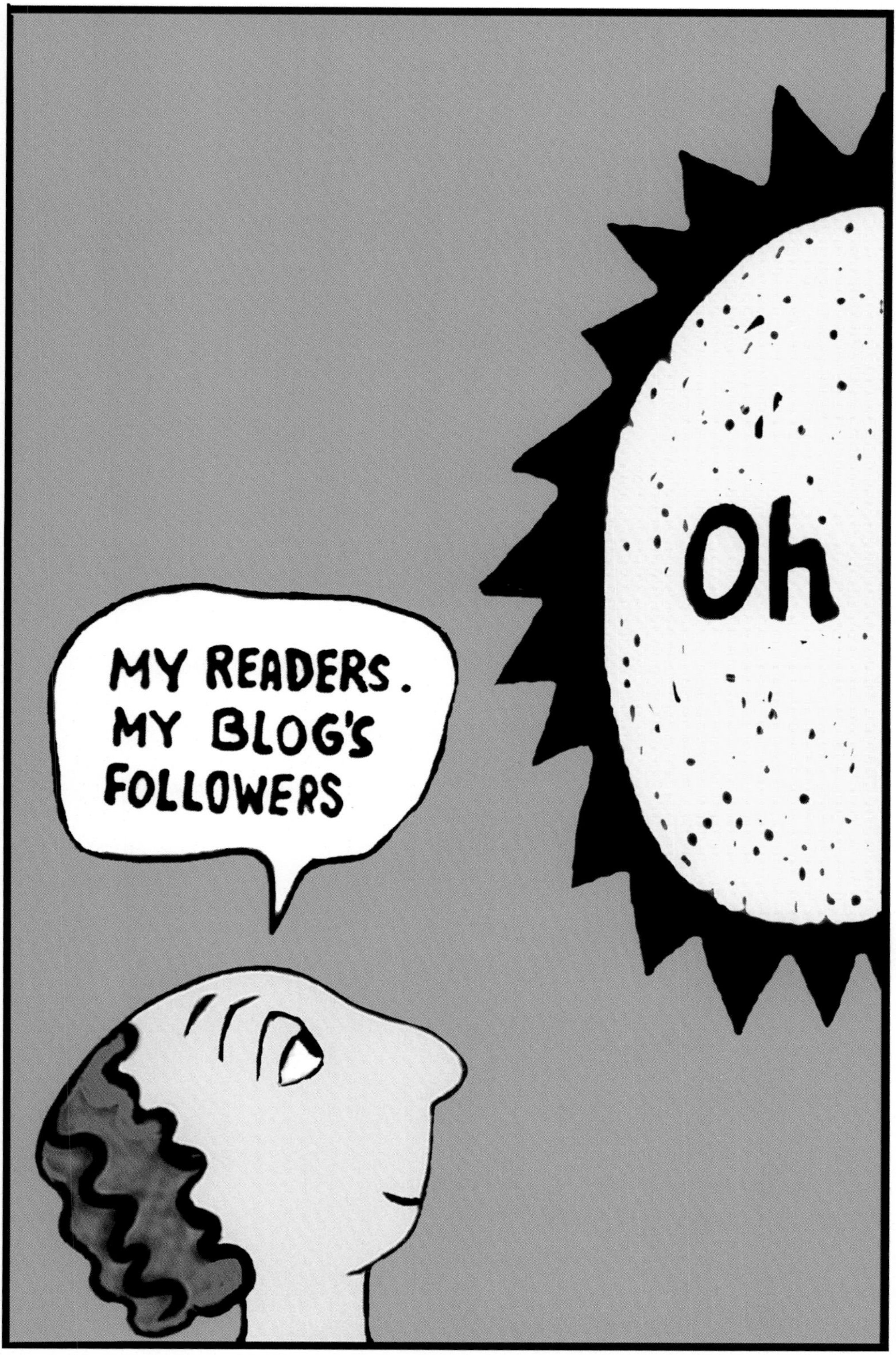
Oh
MY READERS.
MY BLOG'S
FOLLOWERS

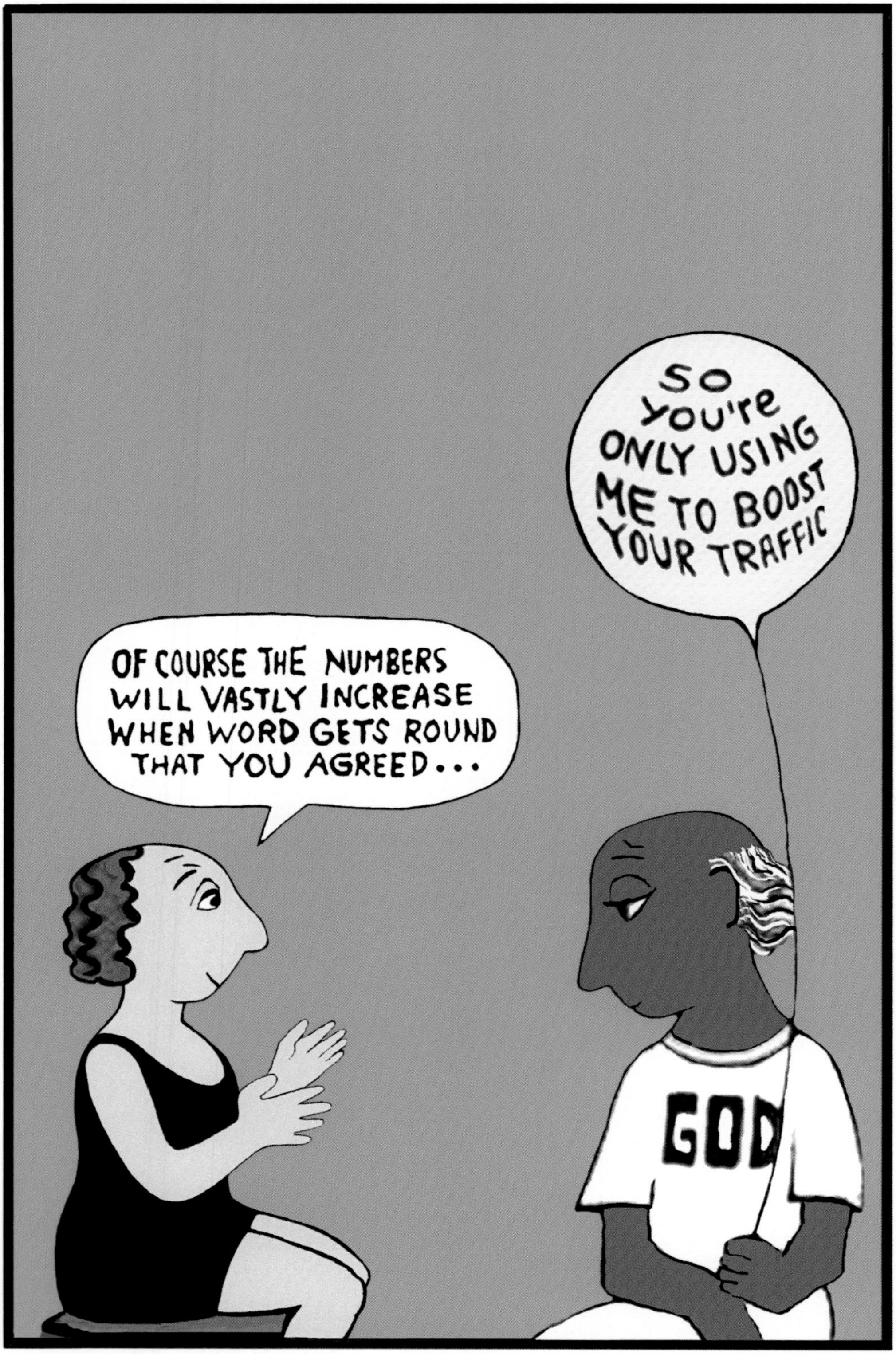
SO YOU'RE ONLY USING ME TO BOOST YOUR TRAFFIC
OF COURSE THE NUMBERS WILL VASTLY INCREASE WHEN WORD GETS ROUND THAT YOU AGREED...
GOD

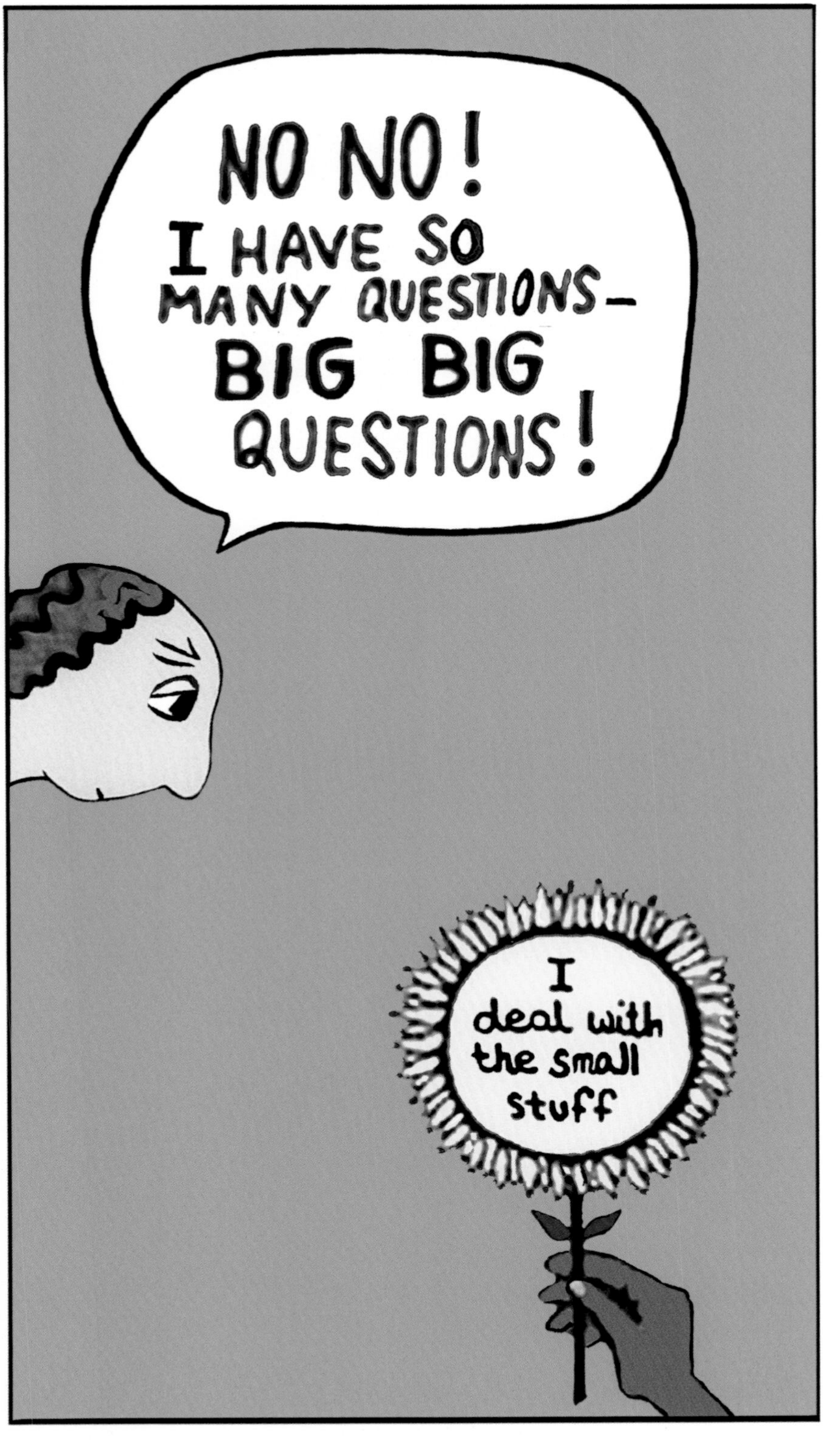
NO NO!
I HAVE SO MANY QUESTIONS– BIG BIG QUESTIONS!
I deal with the small stuff

TWO

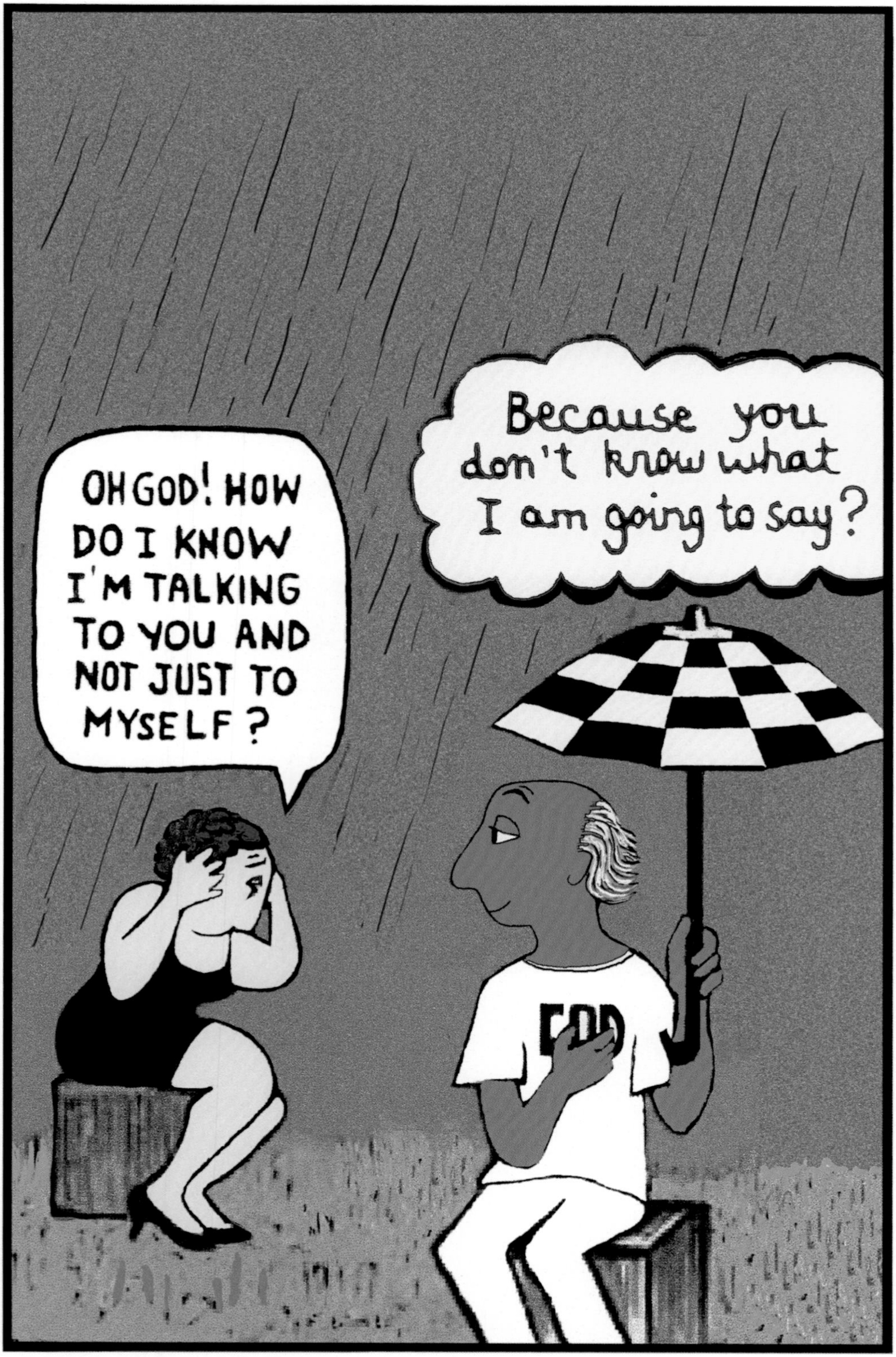
OH GOD! HOW DO I KNOW I'M TALKING TO YOU AND NOT JUST TO MYSELF?
Because you don't know what I am going to say?

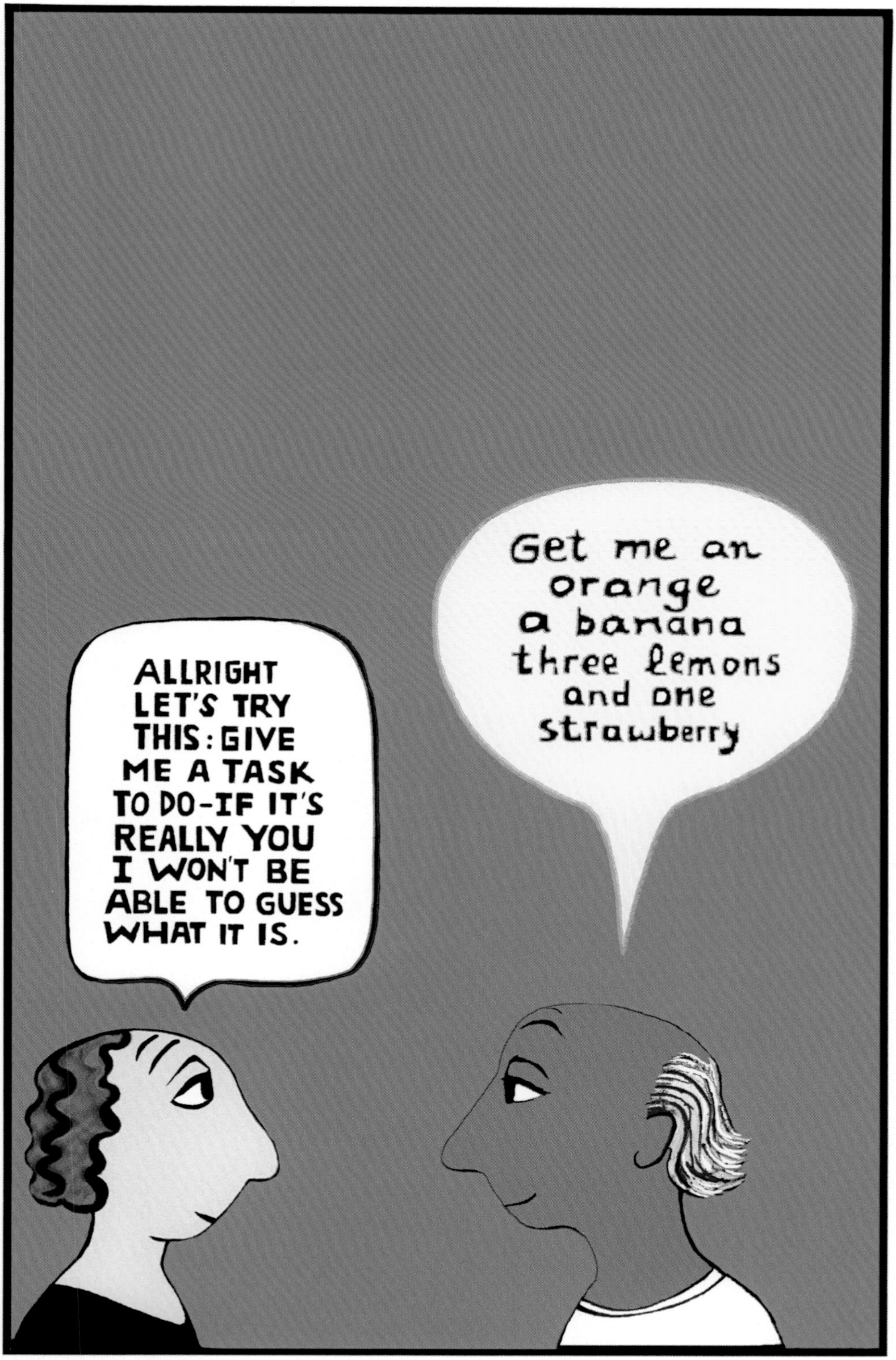
ALLRIGHT LET'S TRY THIS: GIVE ME A TASK TO DO-IF IT'S REALLY YOU I WON'T BE ABLE TO GUESS WHAT IT IS.
Get me an orange a banana three lemons and one strawberry

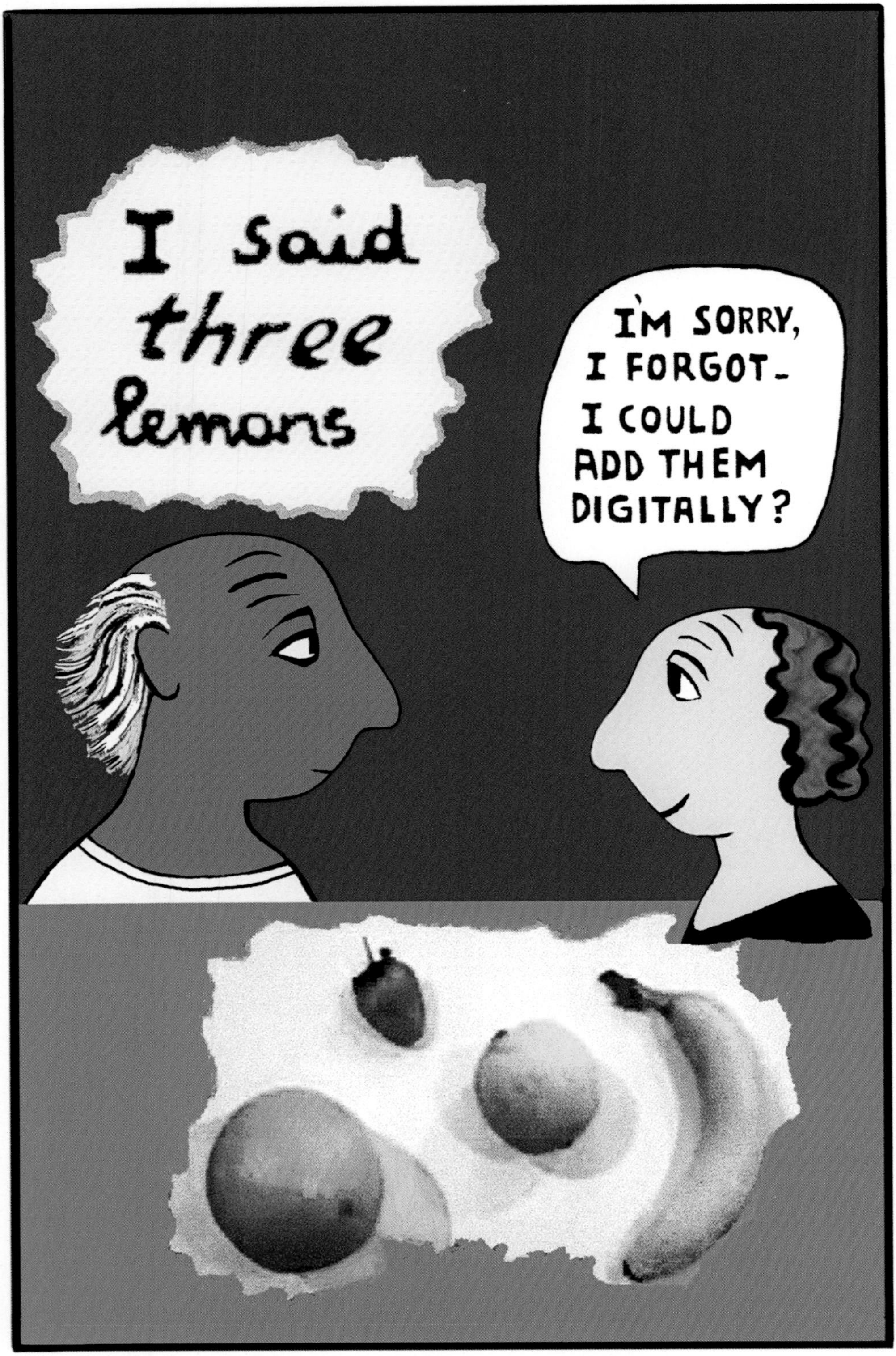
I said three lemons
I'M SORRY, I FORGOT - I COULD ADD THEM DIGITALLY?

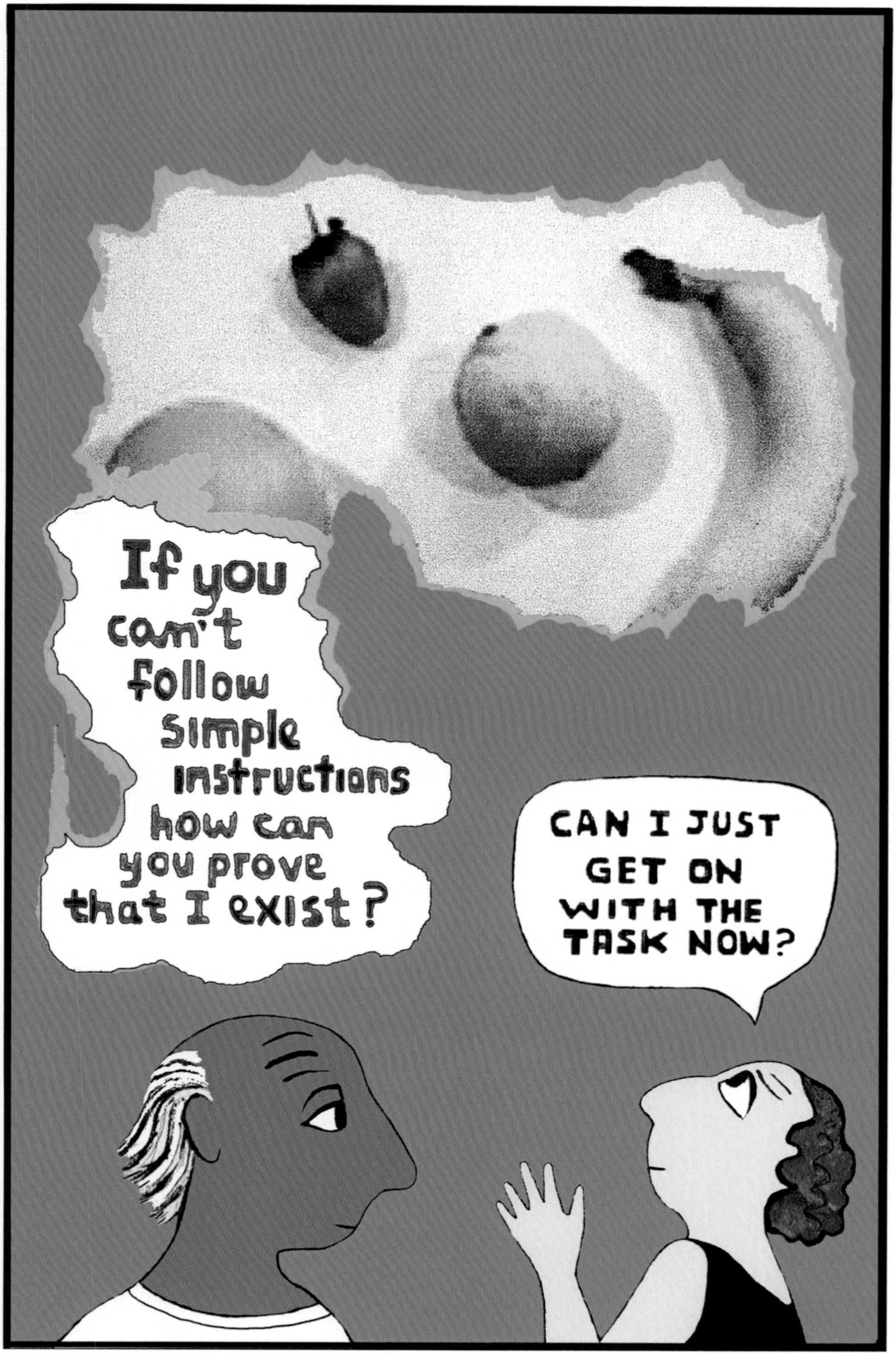
If you can't follow simple instructions how can you prove that I exist?
CAN I JUST GET ON WITH THE TASK NOW?

THREE

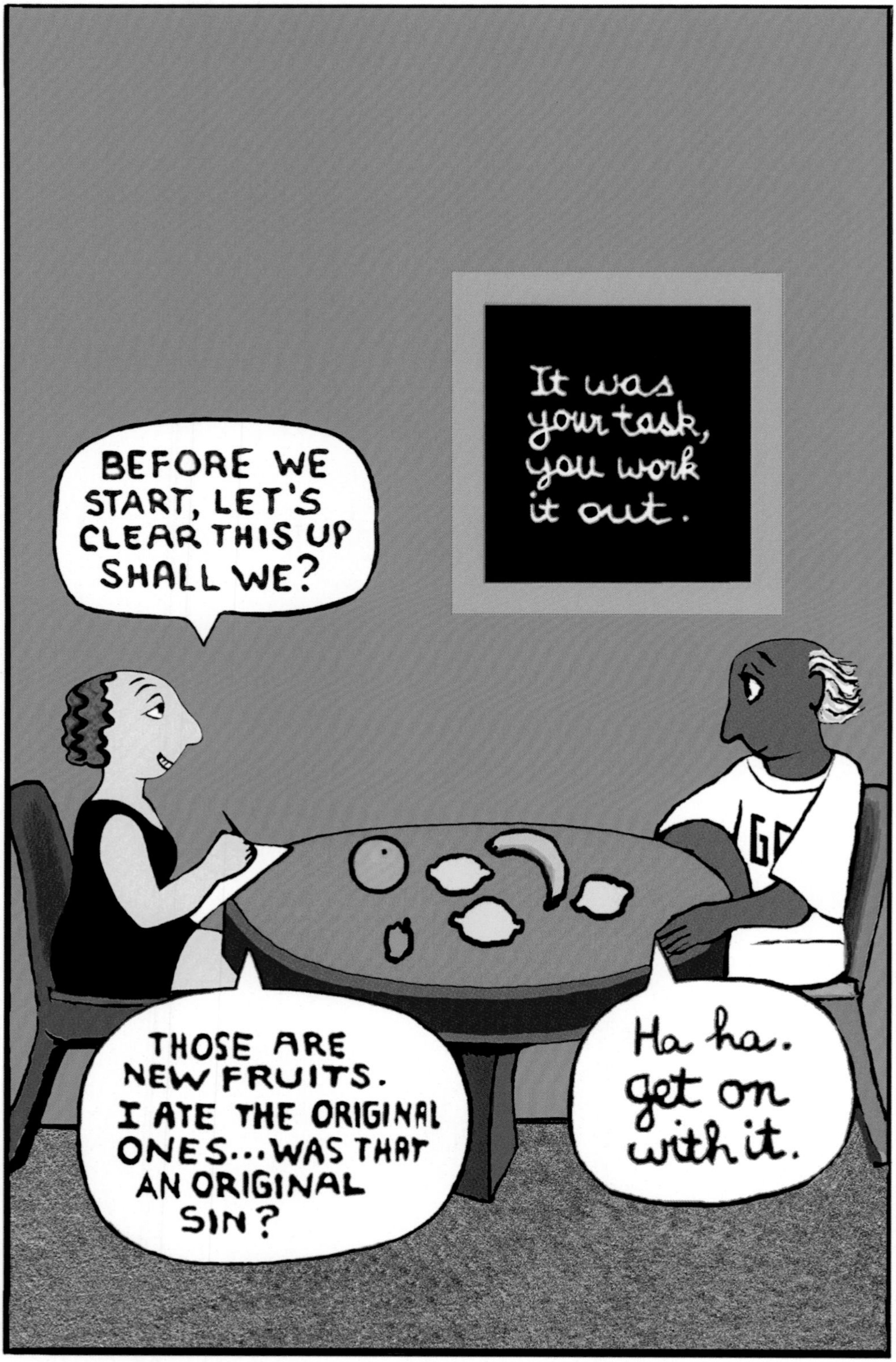
It was your task, you work it out.
BEFORE WE START, LET'S CLEAR THIS UP SHALL WE?
THOSE ARE NEW FRUITS. I ATE THE ORIGINAL ONES...WAS THAT AN ORIGINAL SIN?
Ha ha. get on with it.

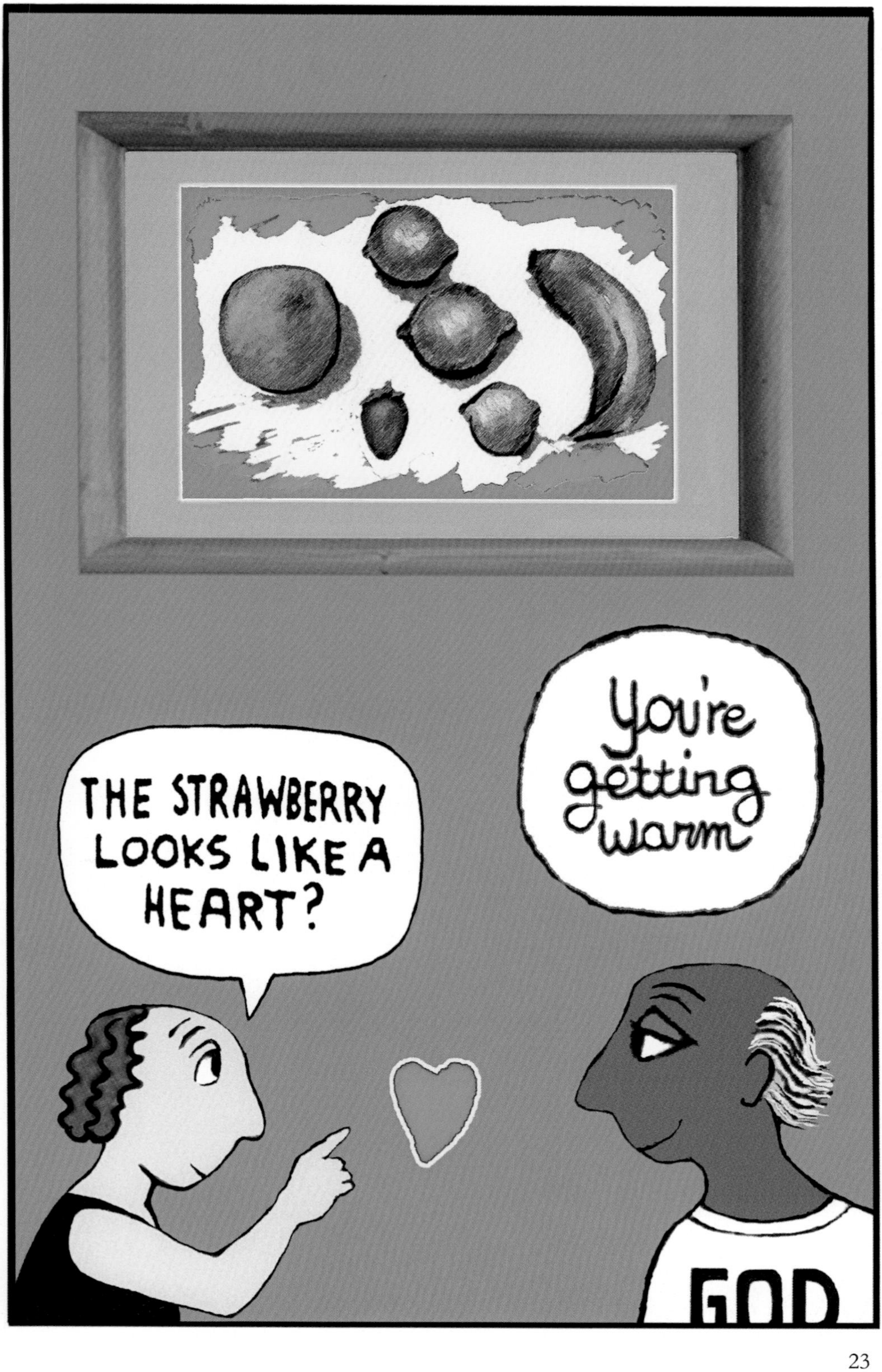
THE STRAWBERRY LOOKS LIKE A HEART?
You're getting warm
GOD

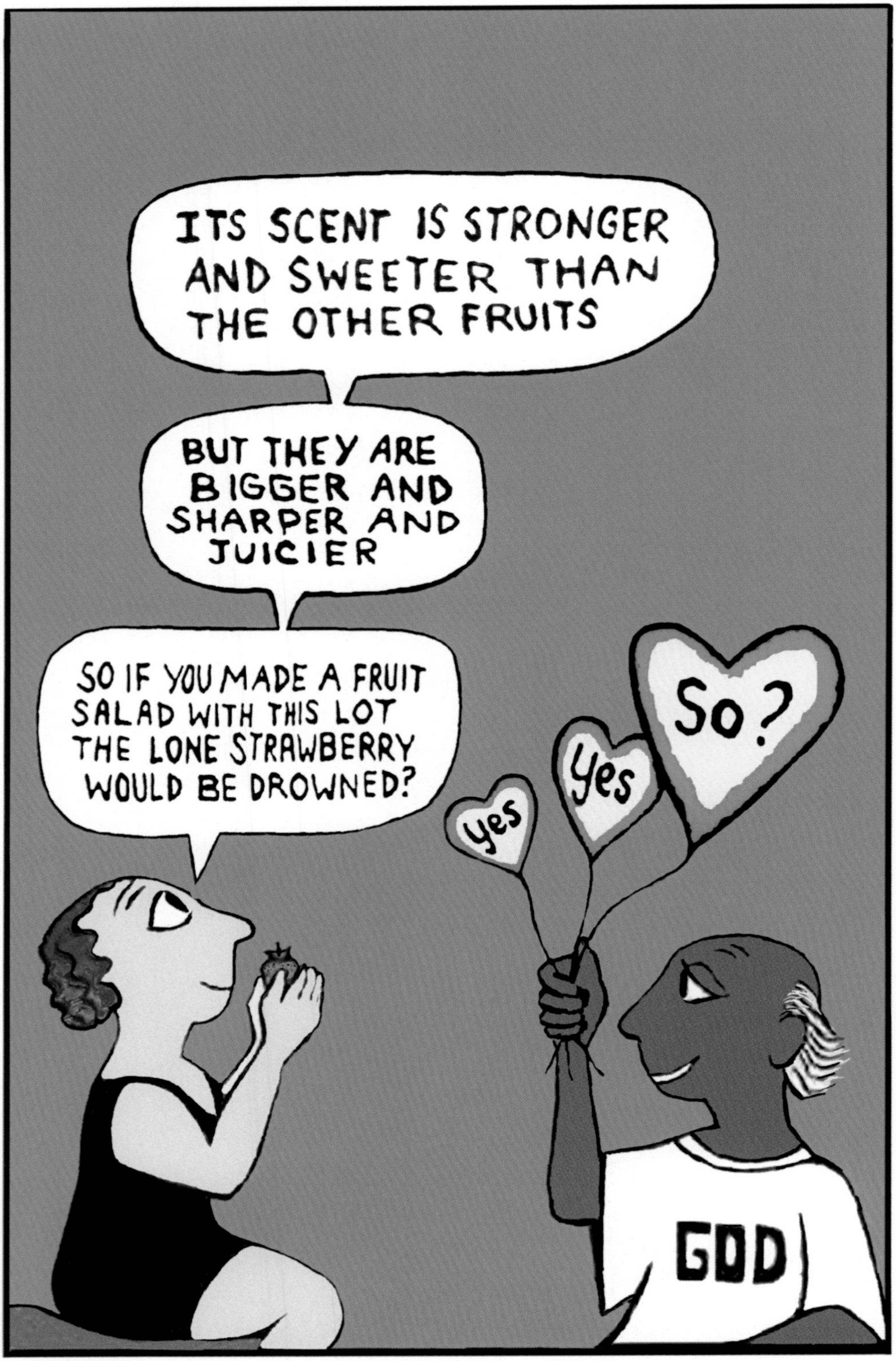
ITS SCENT IS STRONGER AND SWEETER THAN THE OTHER FRUITS
BUT THEY ARE BIGGER AND SHARPER AND JUICIER
SO IF YOU MADE A FRUIT SALAD WITH THIS LOT THE LONE STRAWBERRY WOULD BE DROWNED?
yes
yes
So?
GOD

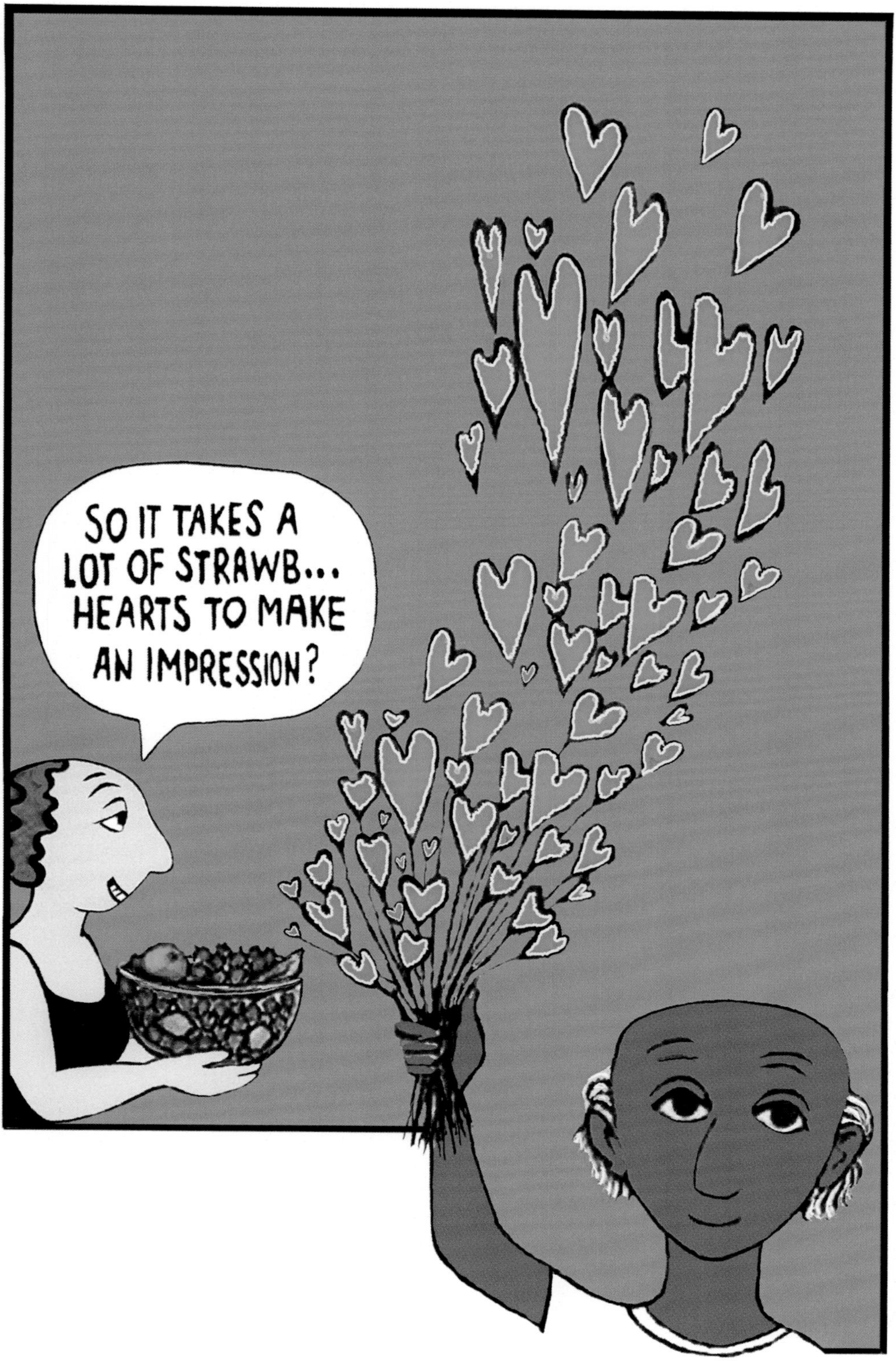
SO IT TAKES A LOT OF STRAWB... HEARTS TO MAKE AN IMPRESSION?

FOUR

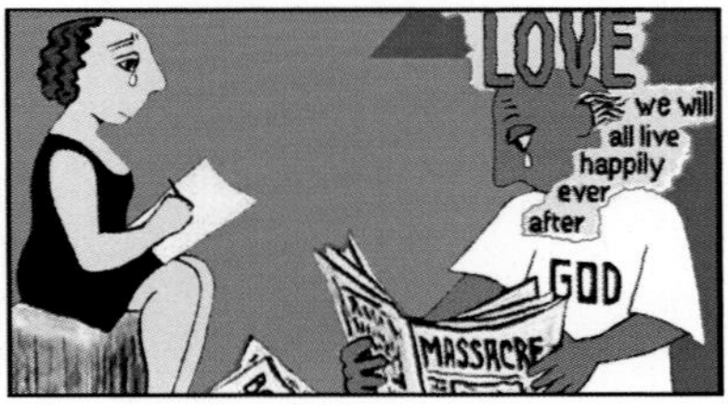
LOVE
we will
all live
happily
ever
after
GOD
MASSACRE

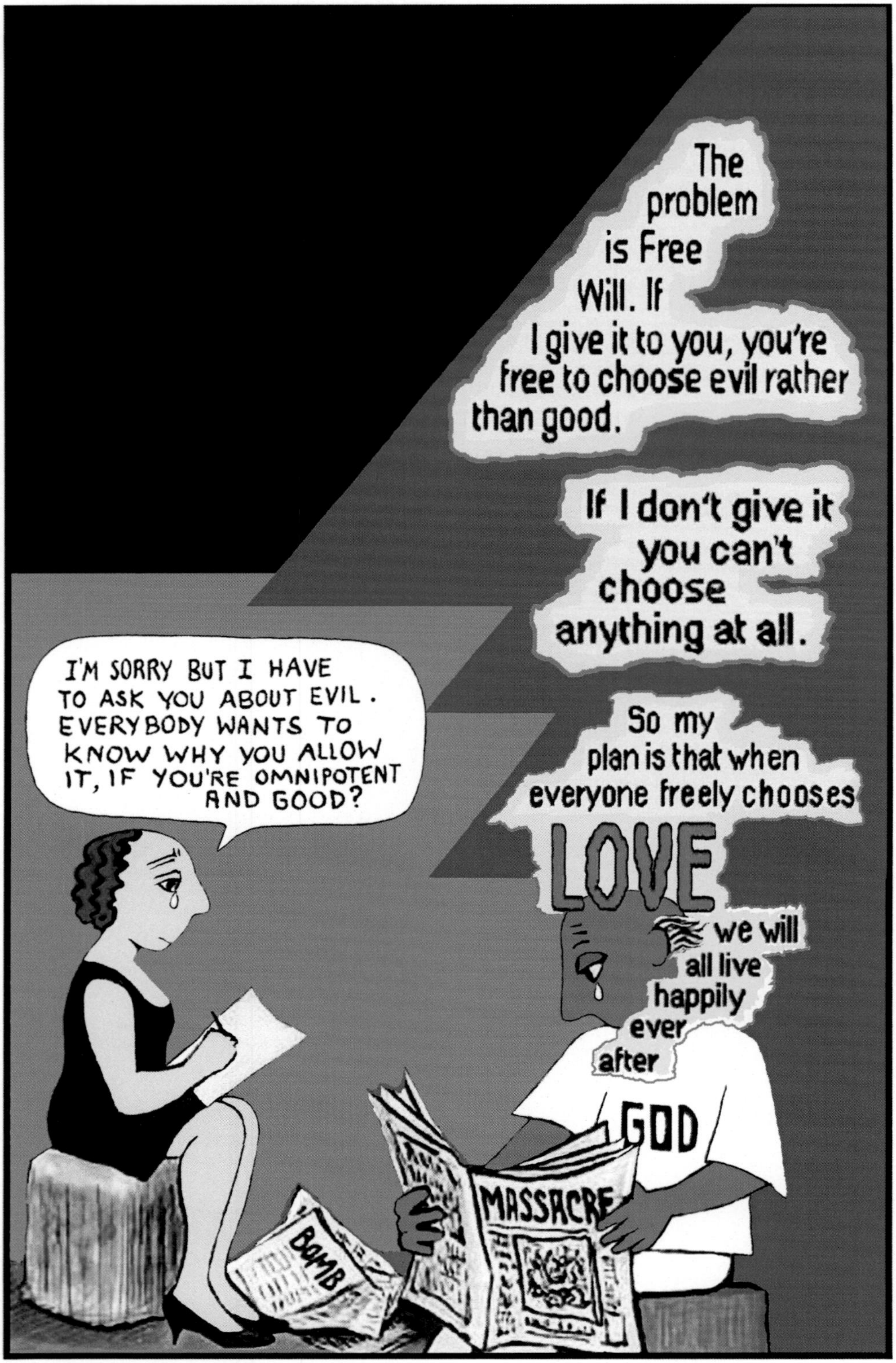
The problem is Free Will. If I give it to you, you're free to choose evil rather than good.
If I don't give it you can't choose anything at all.
I'M SORRY BUT I HAVE TO ASK YOU ABOUT EVIL. EVERYBODY WANTS TO KNOW WHY YOU ALLOW IT, IF YOU'RE OMNIPOTENT AND GOOD?
So my plan is that when everyone freely chooses LOVE we will all live happily ever after
GOD
MASSACRE
BOMB

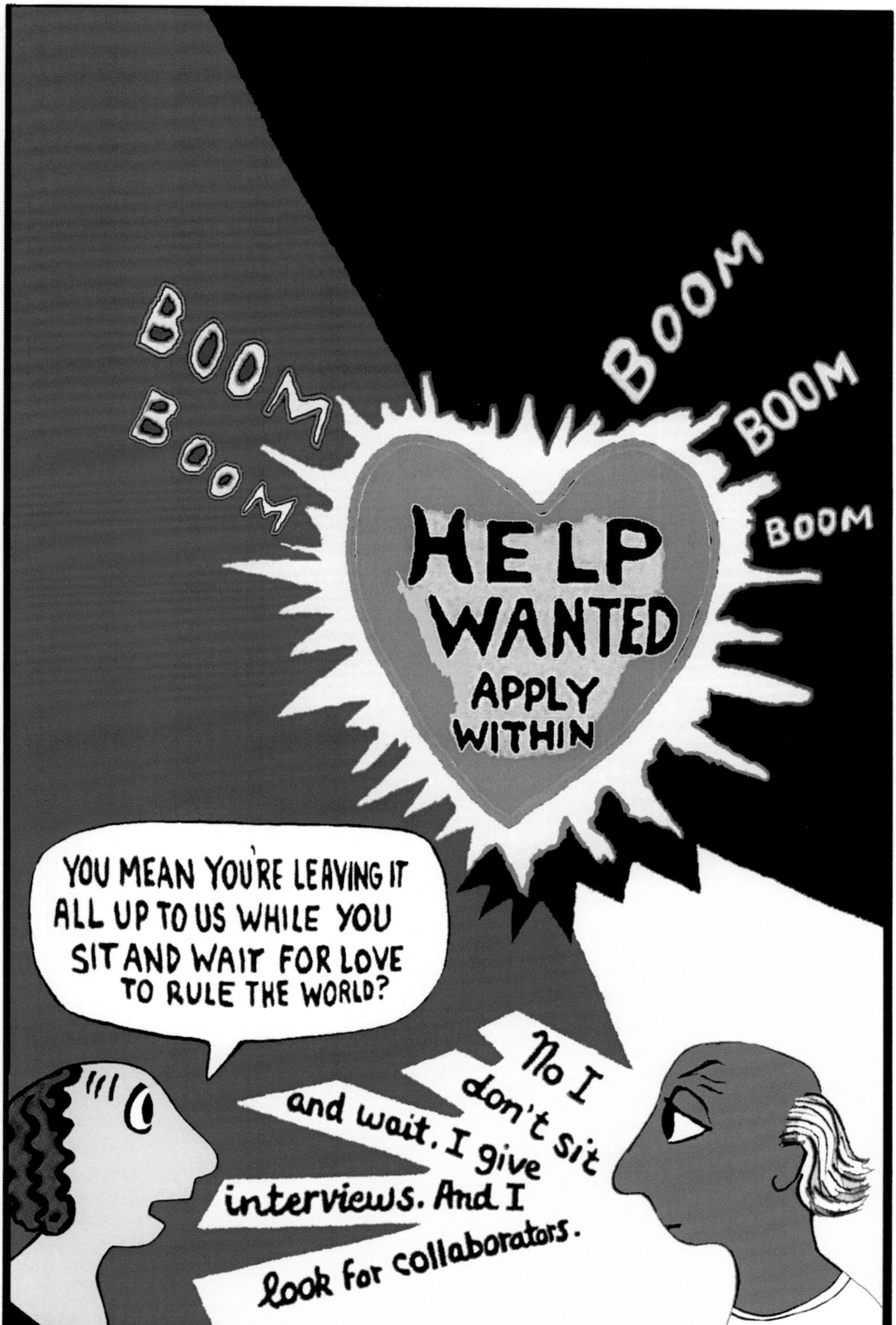
BOOM BOOM
BOOM BOOM BOOM
HELP WANTED APPLY WITHIN
YOU MEAN YOU'RE LEAVING IT ALL UP TO US WHILE YOU SIT AND WAIT FOR LOVE TO RULE THE WORLD?
No I don't sit and wait. I give interviews. And I look for collaborators.

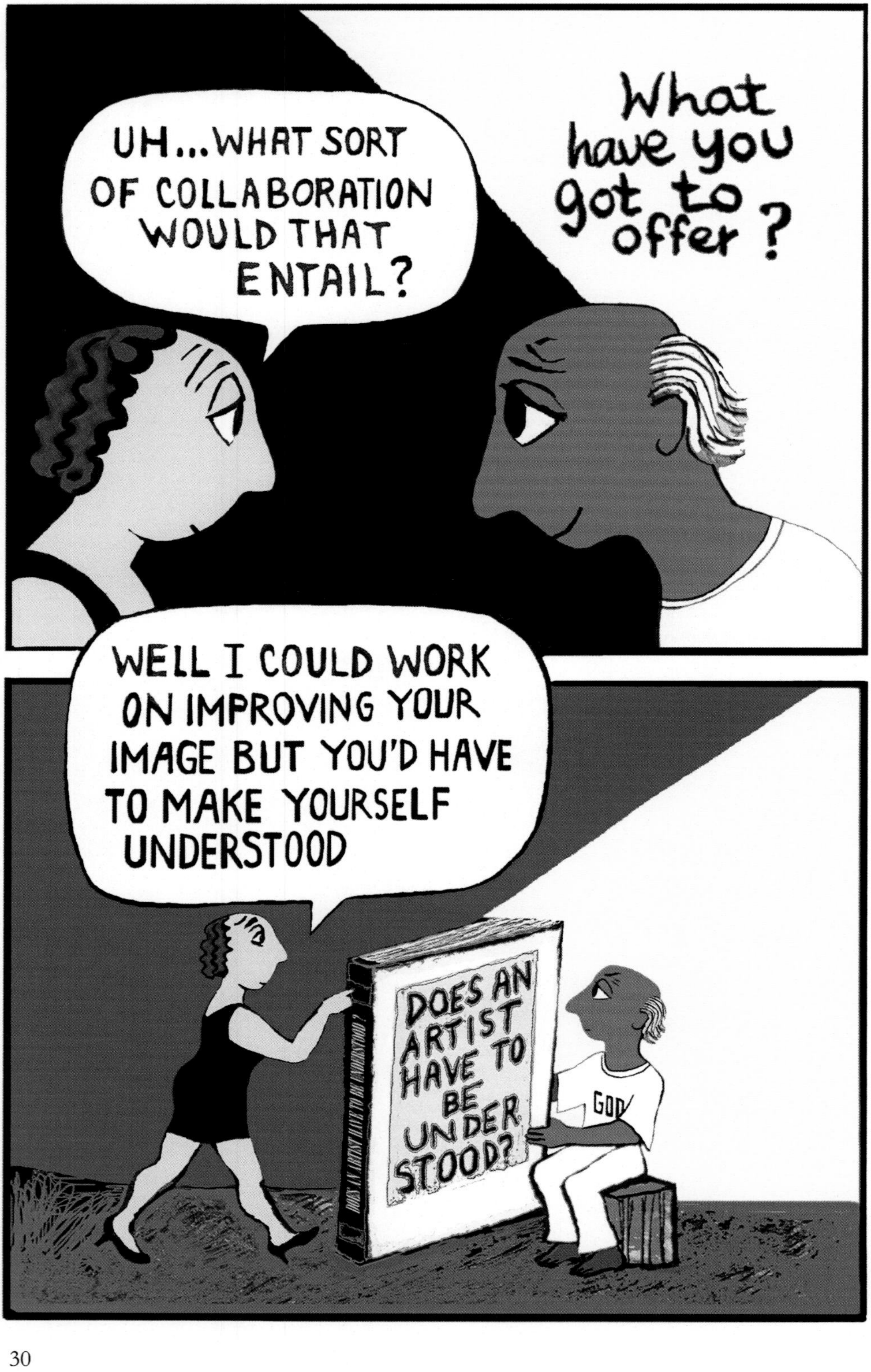
UH...WHAT SORT OF COLLABORATION WOULD THAT ENTAIL?
What have you got to offer?
WELL I COULD WORK ON IMPROVING YOUR IMAGE BUT YOU'D HAVE TO MAKE YOURSELF UNDERSTOOD
DOES AN ARTIST HAVE TO BE UNDER STOOD?
GOD

FIVE

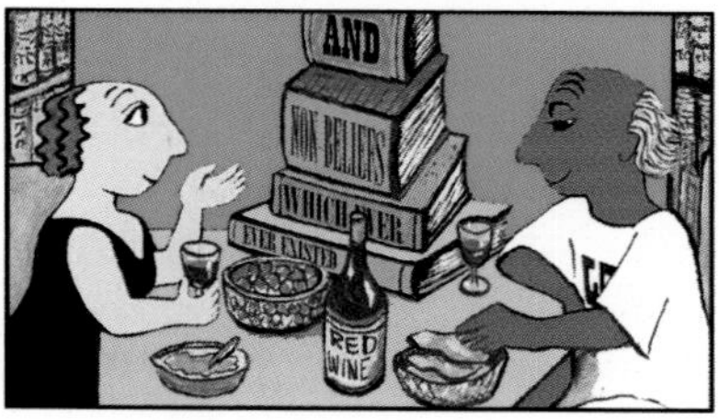
AND
NON BELIEFS
EVER EXISTED
RED
WINE

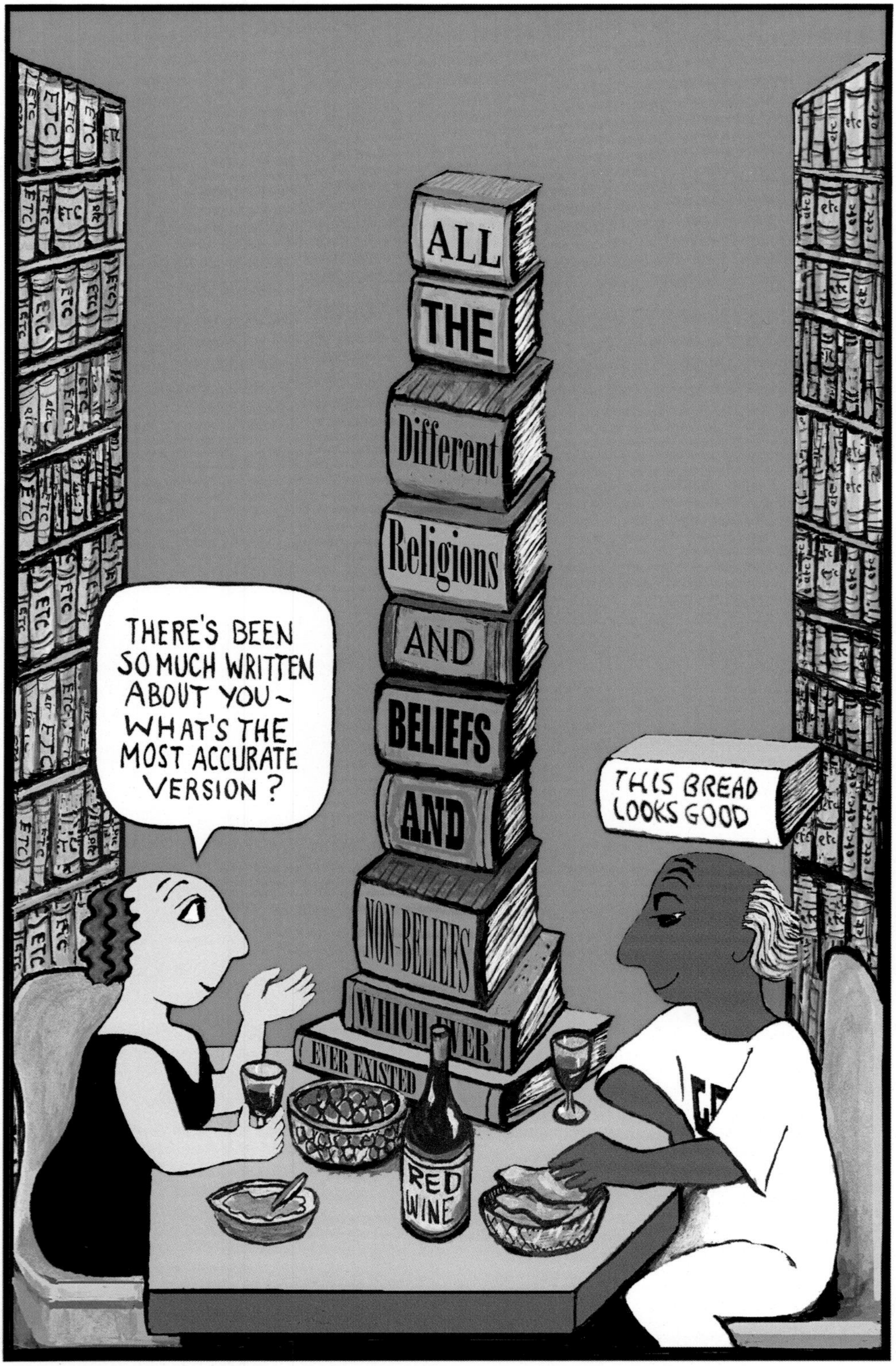
ALL
THE
Different
Religions
AND
BELIEFS
AND
NON-BELIEFS
WHICH VER
EVER EXISTED
THERE'S BEEN SO MUCH WRITTEN ABOUT YOU~ WHAT'S THE MOST ACCURATE VERSION?
THIS BREAD LOOKS GOOD
RED WINE

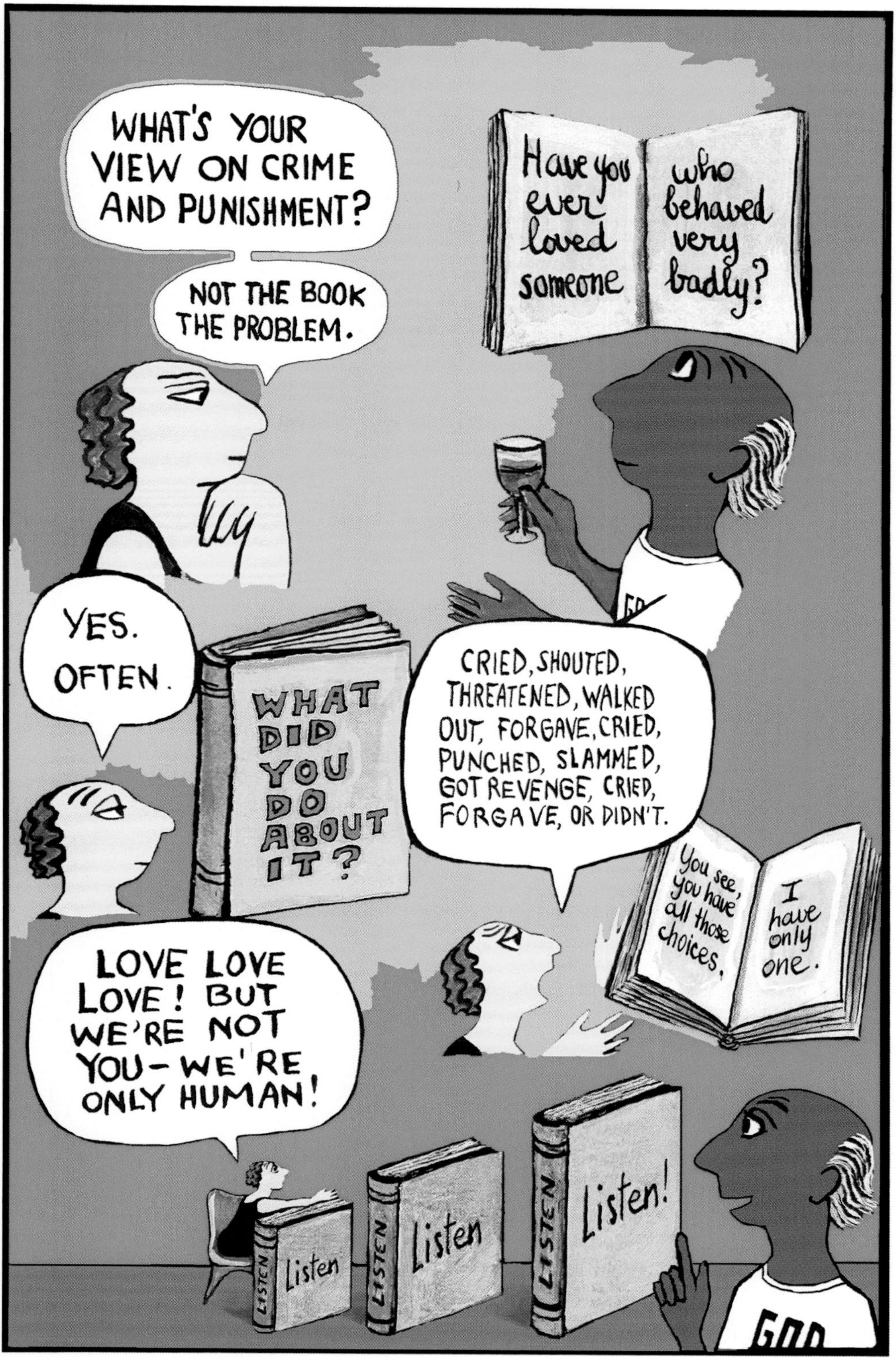
WHAT'S YOUR VIEW ON CRIME AND PUNISHMENT?
NOT THE BOOK THE PROBLEM.
Have you ever loved someone
who behaved very badly?
YES. OFTEN.
WHAT DID YOU DO ABOUT IT?
CRIED, SHOUTED, THREATENED, WALKED OUT, FORGAVE, CRIED, PUNCHED, SLAMMED, GOT REVENGE, CRIED, FORGAVE, OR DIDN'T.
You see, you have all those choices,
I have only one.
LOVE LOVE LOVE! BUT WE'RE NOT YOU - WE'RE ONLY HUMAN!
LISTEN
Listen
LISTEN
Listen
LISTEN
Listen!

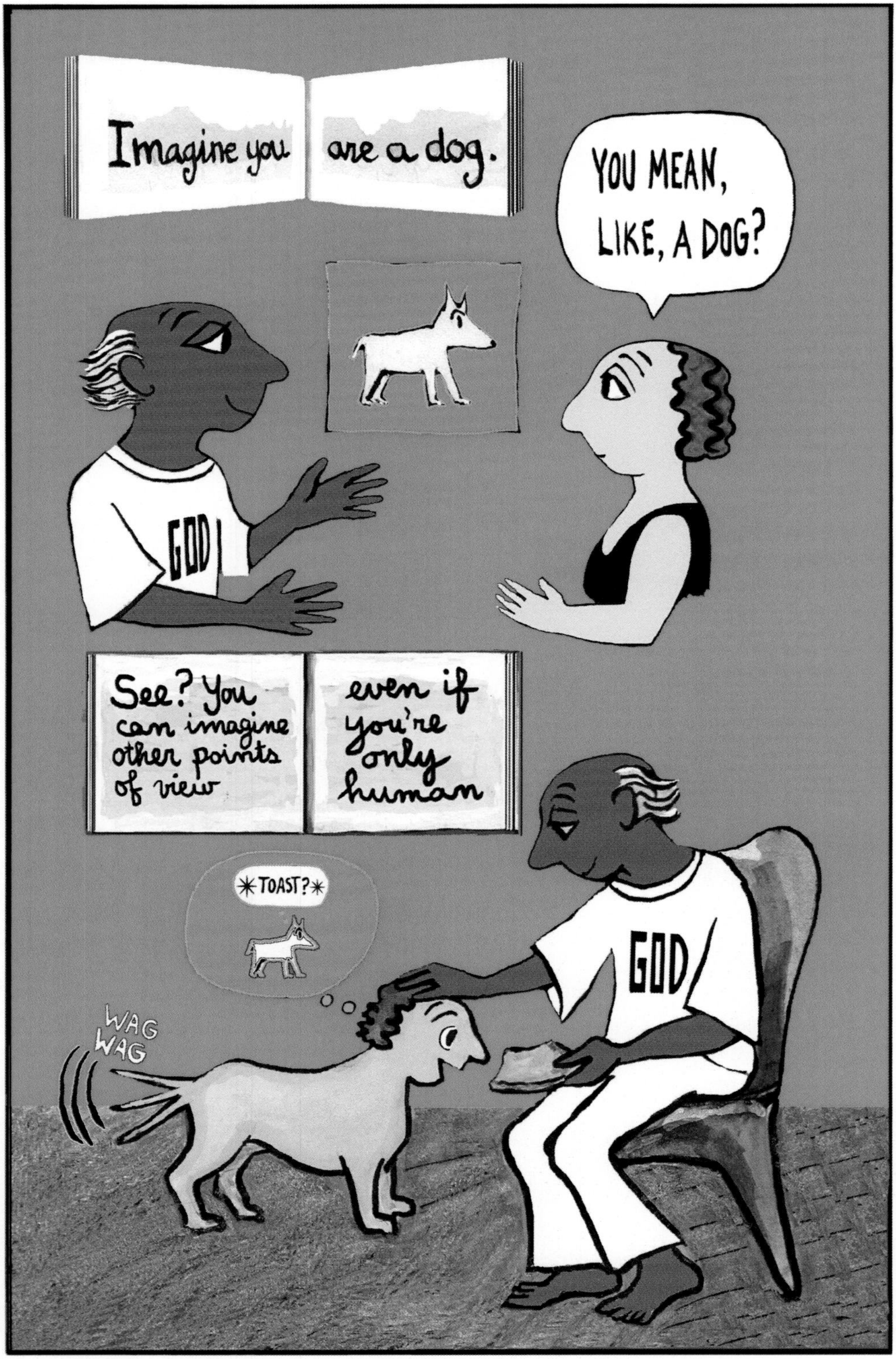

Imagine you are a dog.
YOU MEAN, LIKE, A DOG?
GOD
See? You can imagine other points of view even if you're only human
TOAST?
WAG WAG
GOD

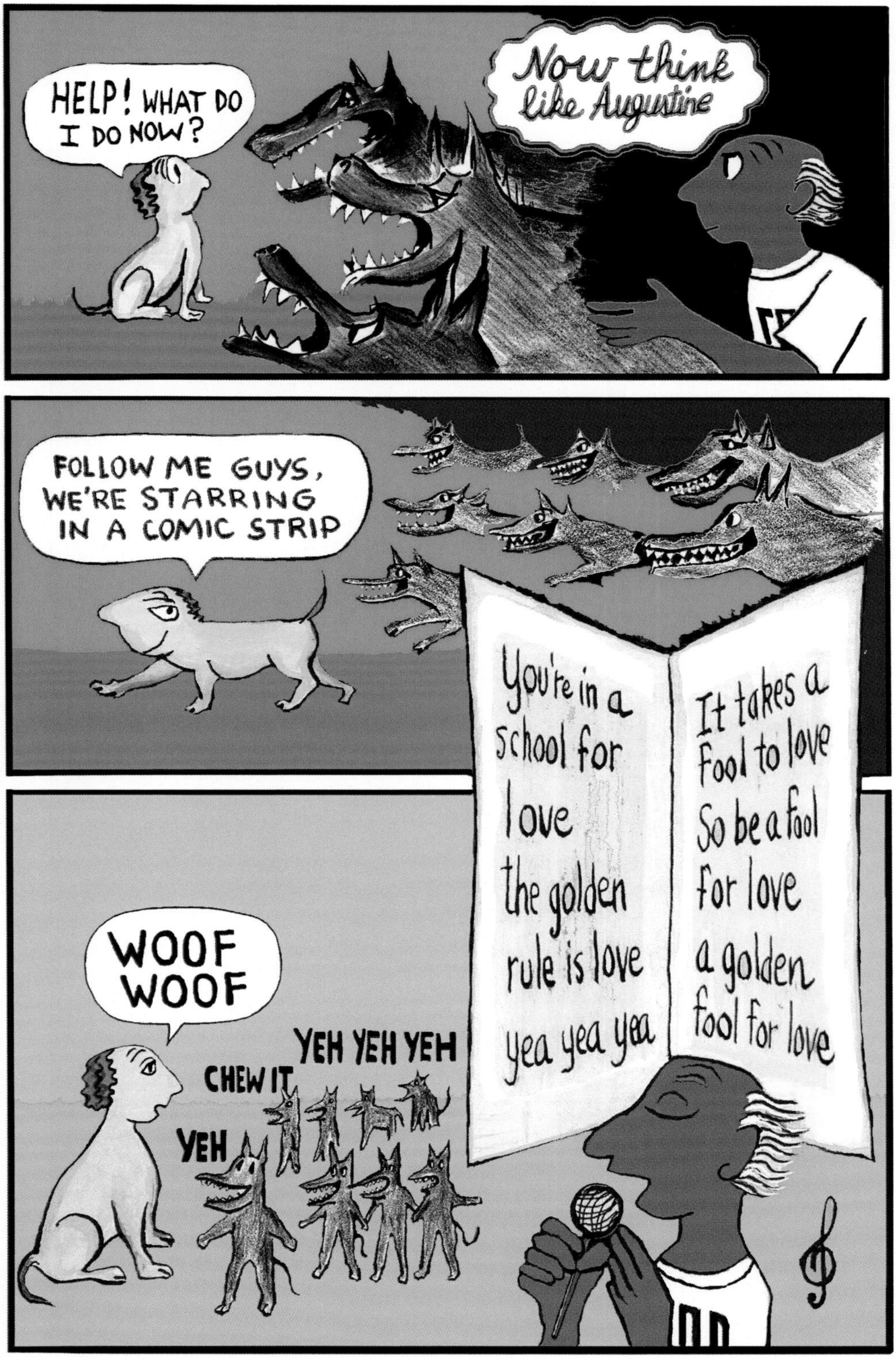
HELP! WHAT DO I DO NOW?
Now think like Augustine
FOLLOW ME GUYS, WE'RE STARRING IN A COMIC STRIP
You're in a school for love the golden rule is love yea yea yea
It takes a Fool to love So be a fool for love a golden fool for love
WOOF WOOF
YEH YEH YEH
CHEW IT
YEH

SIX

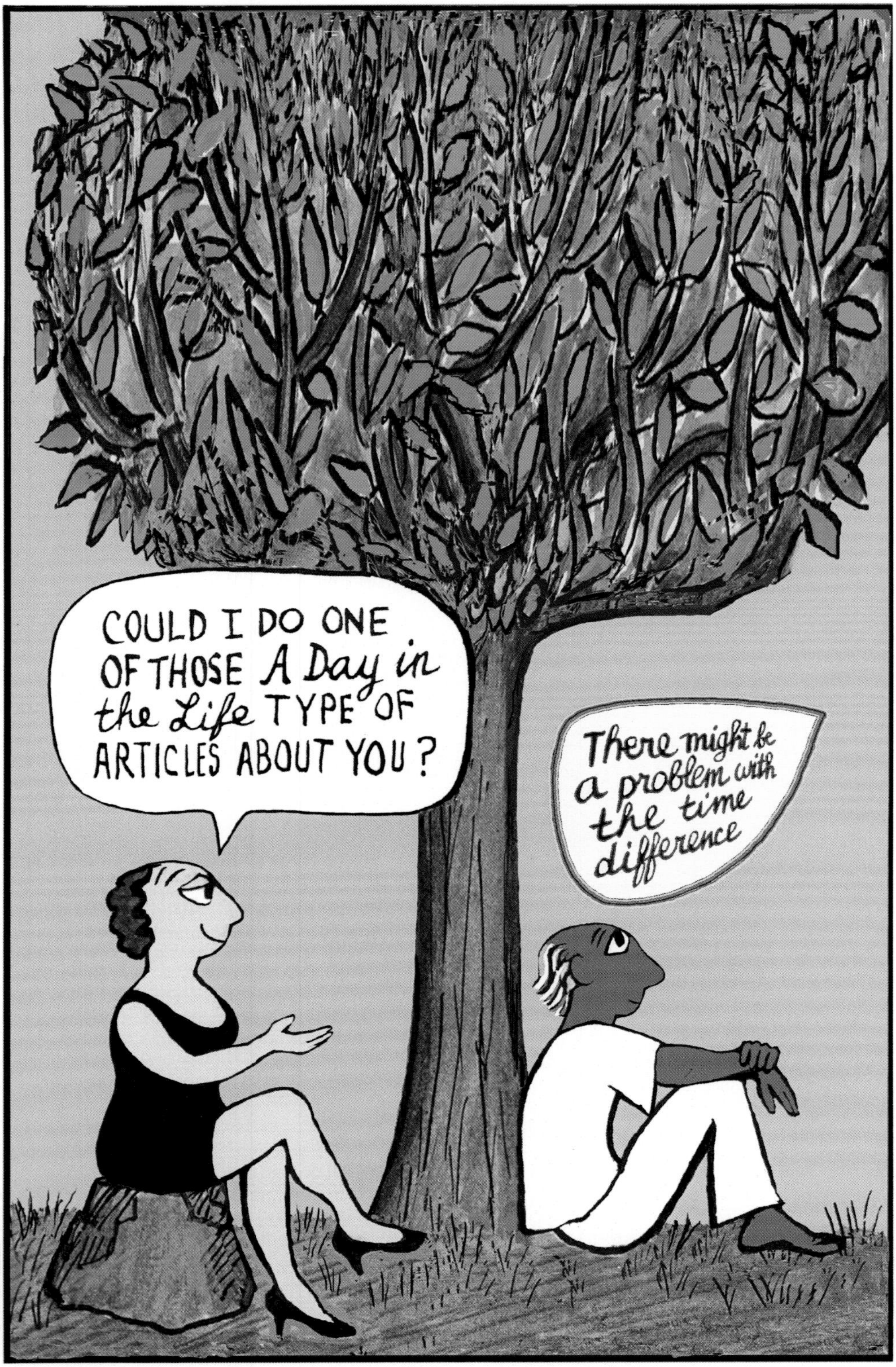
COULD I DO ONE OF THOSE *A Day in the Life* TYPE OF ARTICLES ABOUT YOU?
There might be a problem with the time difference

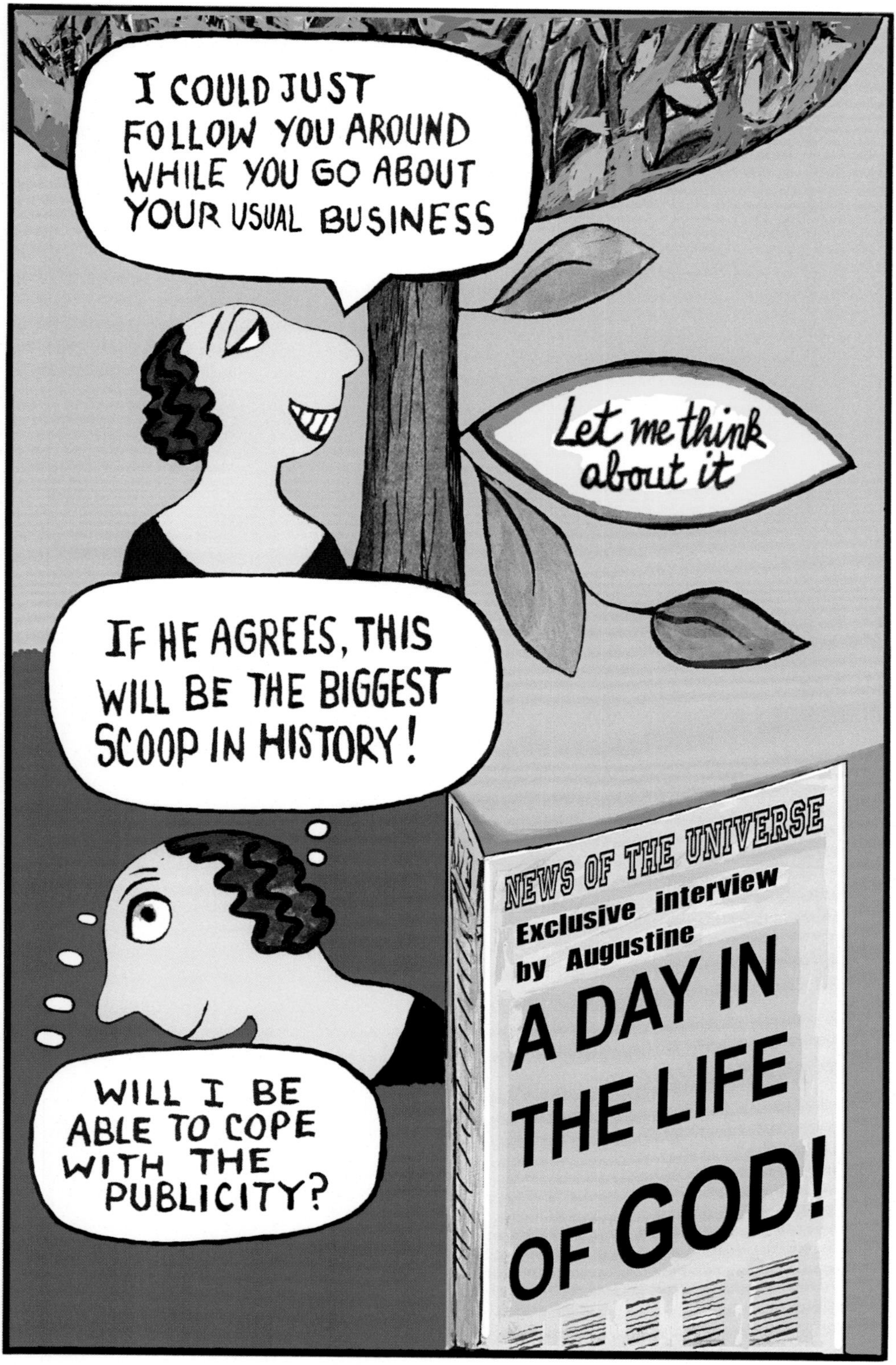
I COULD JUST FOLLOW YOU AROUND WHILE YOU GO ABOUT YOUR USUAL BUSINESS
Let me think about it
IF HE AGREES, THIS WILL BE THE BIGGEST SCOOP IN HISTORY!
WILL I BE ABLE TO COPE WITH THE PUBLICITY?
NEWS OF THE UNIVERSE
Exclusive interview by Augustine
A DAY IN THE LIFE OF GOD!

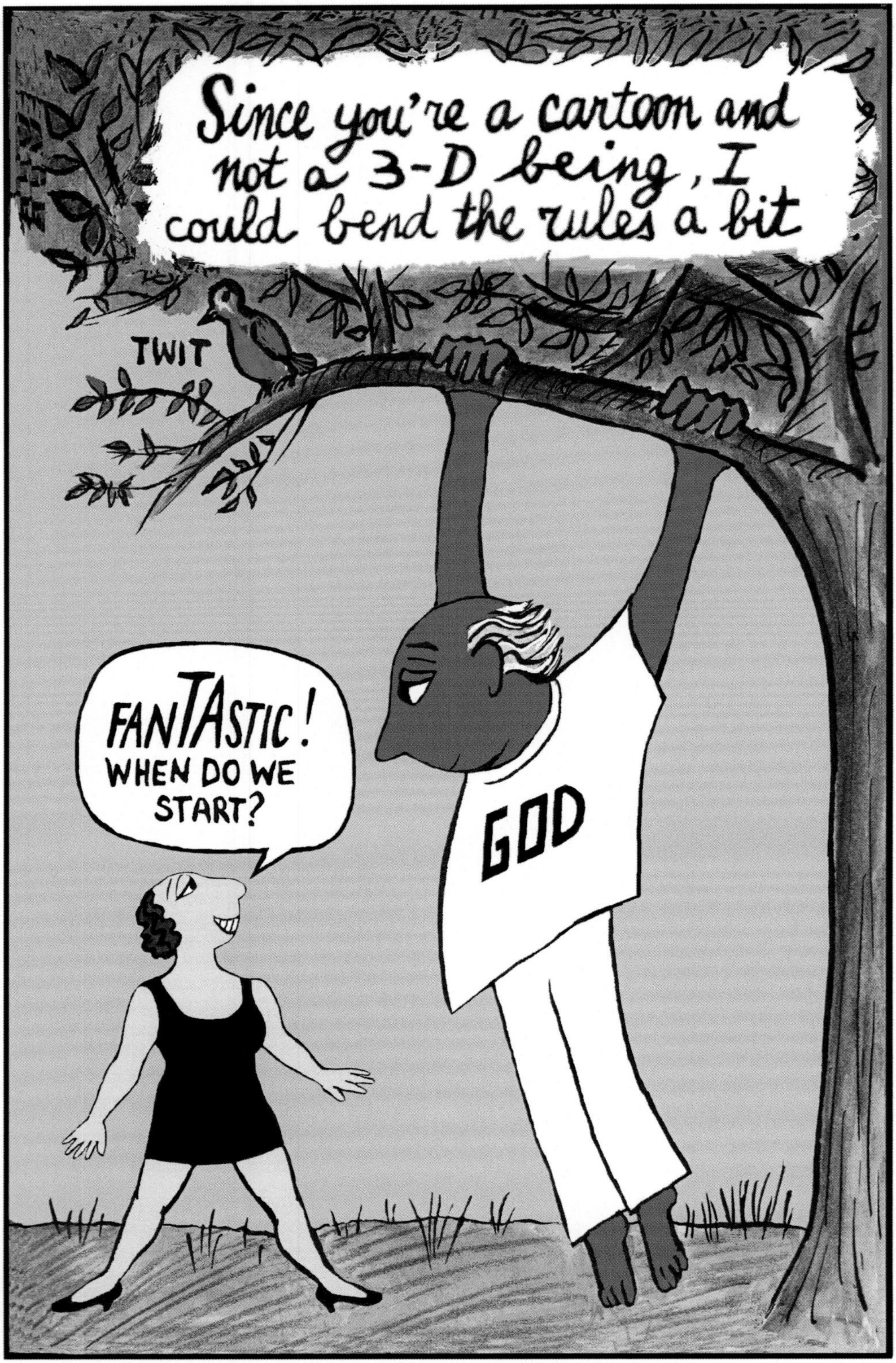
Since you're a cartoon and not a 3-D being, I could bend the rules a bit
TWIT
FANTASTIC! WHEN DO WE START?
GOD

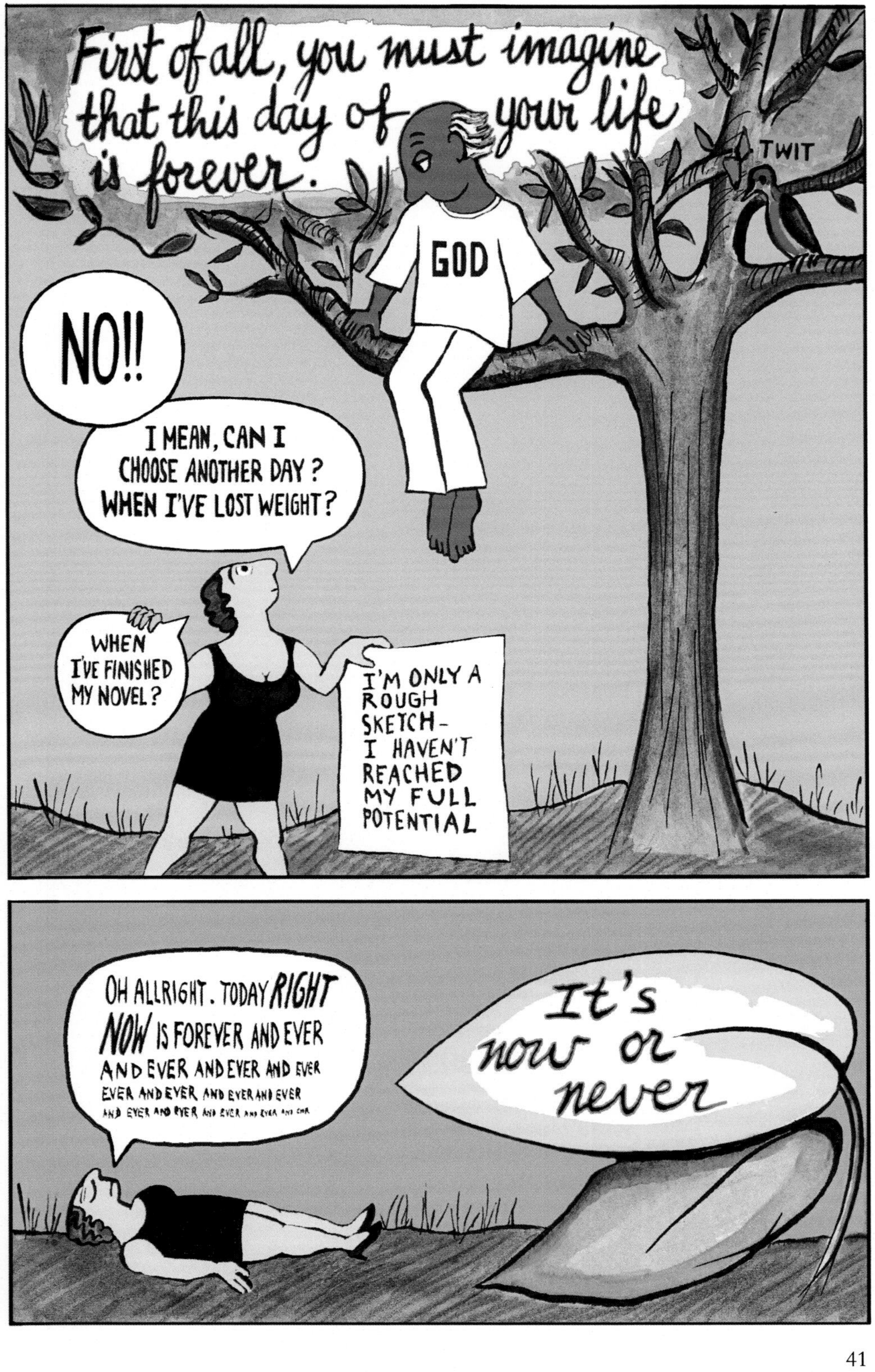
First of all, you must imagine that this day of your life is forever.
GOD
TWIT
NO!!
I MEAN, CAN I CHOOSE ANOTHER DAY? WHEN I'VE LOST WEIGHT?
WHEN I'VE FINISHED MY NOVEL?
I'M ONLY A ROUGH SKETCH- I HAVEN'T REACHED MY FULL POTENTIAL
OH ALLRIGHT. TODAY RIGHT NOW IS FOREVER AND EVER AND EVER AND EVER AND EVER AND EVER EVER AND EVER AND EVER AND EVER
It's now or never

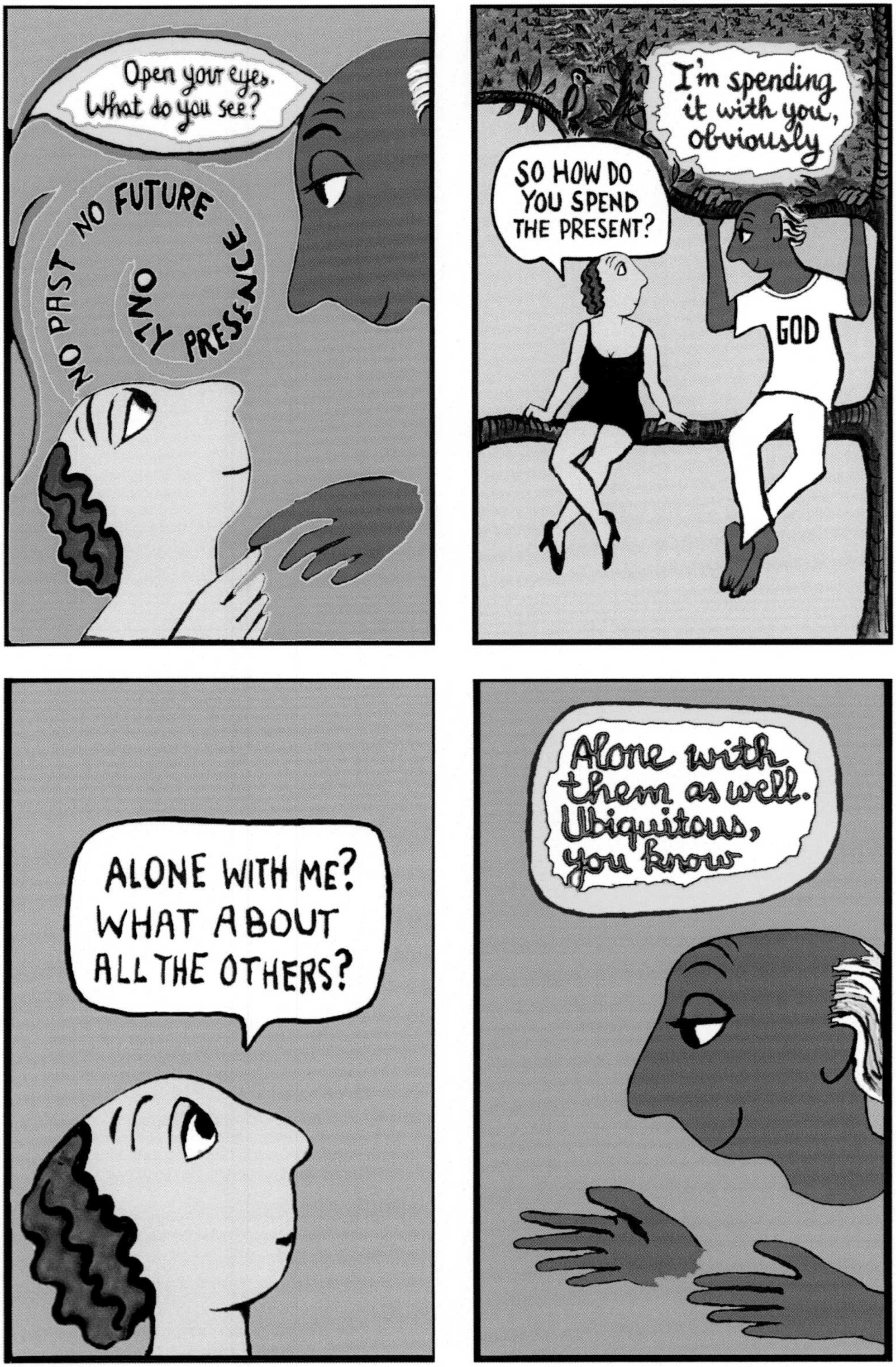

Open your eyes. What do you see?
NO PAST NO FUTURE
ONLY PRESENCE
TWIT
I'm spending it with you, obviously
SO HOW DO YOU SPEND THE PRESENT?
GOD
ALONE WITH ME? WHAT ABOUT ALL THE OTHERS?
Alone with them as well. Ubiquitous, you know

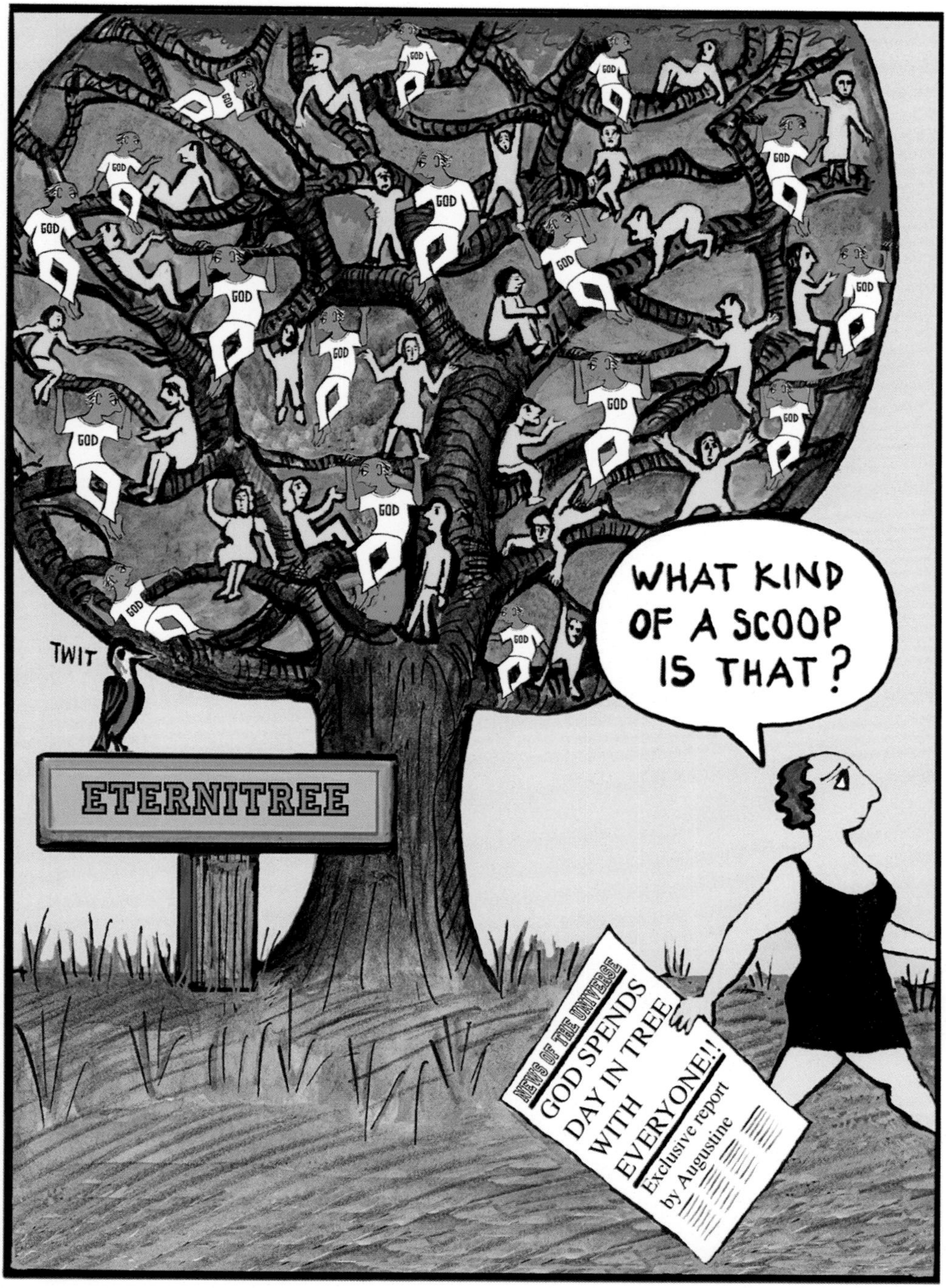

TWIT
ETERNITREE
WHAT KIND OF A SCOOP IS THAT?
NEWS OF THE UNIVERSE
GOD SPENDS DAY IN TREE WITH EVERYONE!!
Exclusive report by Augustine

SEVEN

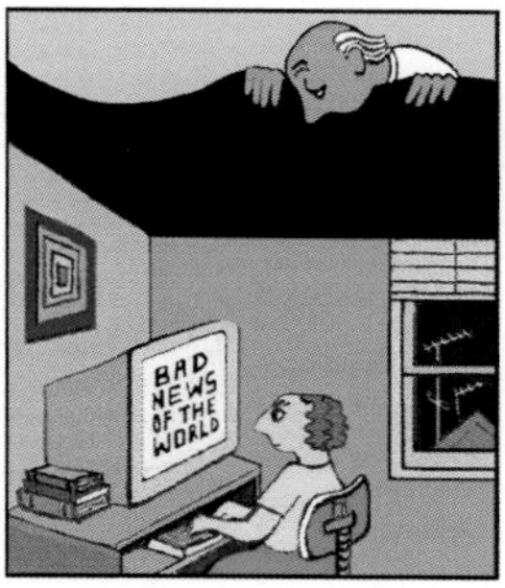
BAD NEWS OF THE WORLD

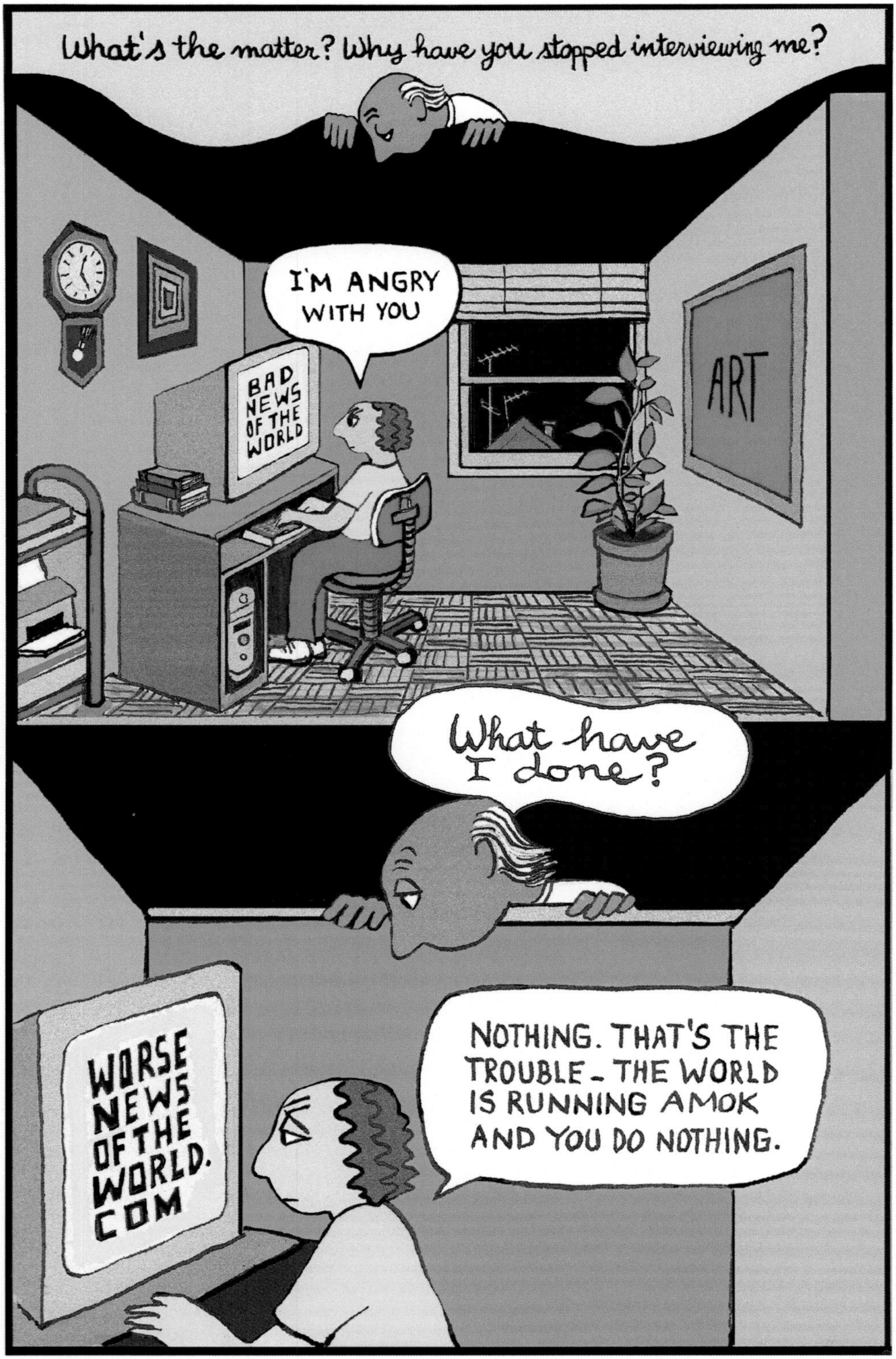
What's the matter? Why have you stopped interviewing me?
I'M ANGRY WITH YOU
BAD NEWS OF THE WORLD
ART
What have I done?
WORSE NEWS OF THE WORLD.COM
NOTHING. THAT'S THE TROUBLE - THE WORLD IS RUNNING AMOK AND YOU DO NOTHING.

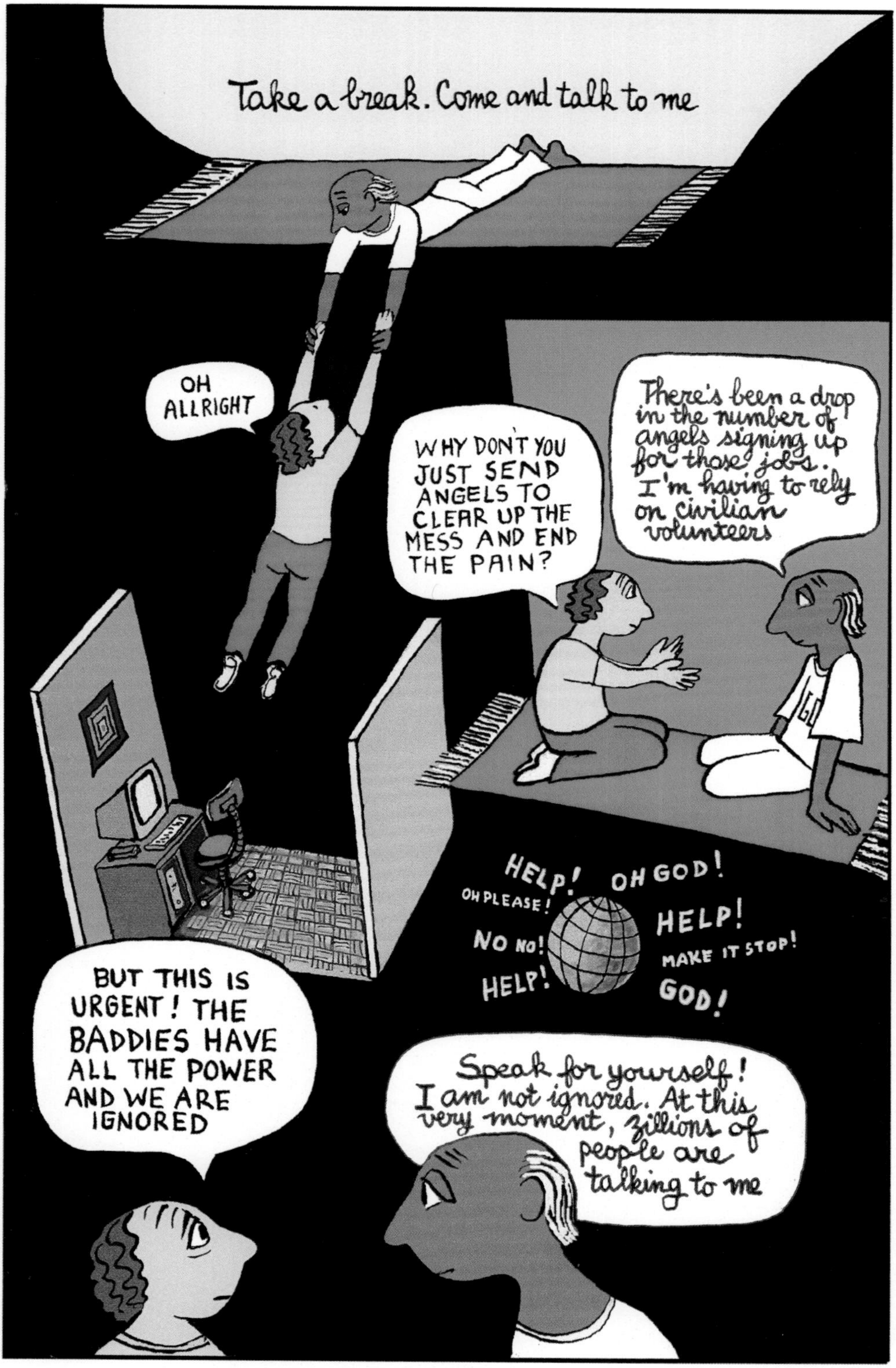
Take a break. Come and talk to me
OH ALLRIGHT
WHY DON'T YOU JUST SEND ANGELS TO CLEAR UP THE MESS AND END THE PAIN?
There's been a drop in the number of angels signing up for those jobs. I'm having to rely on civilian volunteers
HELP! OH GOD!
OH PLEASE!
HELP!
NO NO!
MAKE IT STOP!
HELP!
GOD!
BUT THIS IS URGENT! THE BADDIES HAVE ALL THE POWER AND WE ARE IGNORED
Speak for yourself! I am not ignored. At this very moment, zillions of people are talking to me

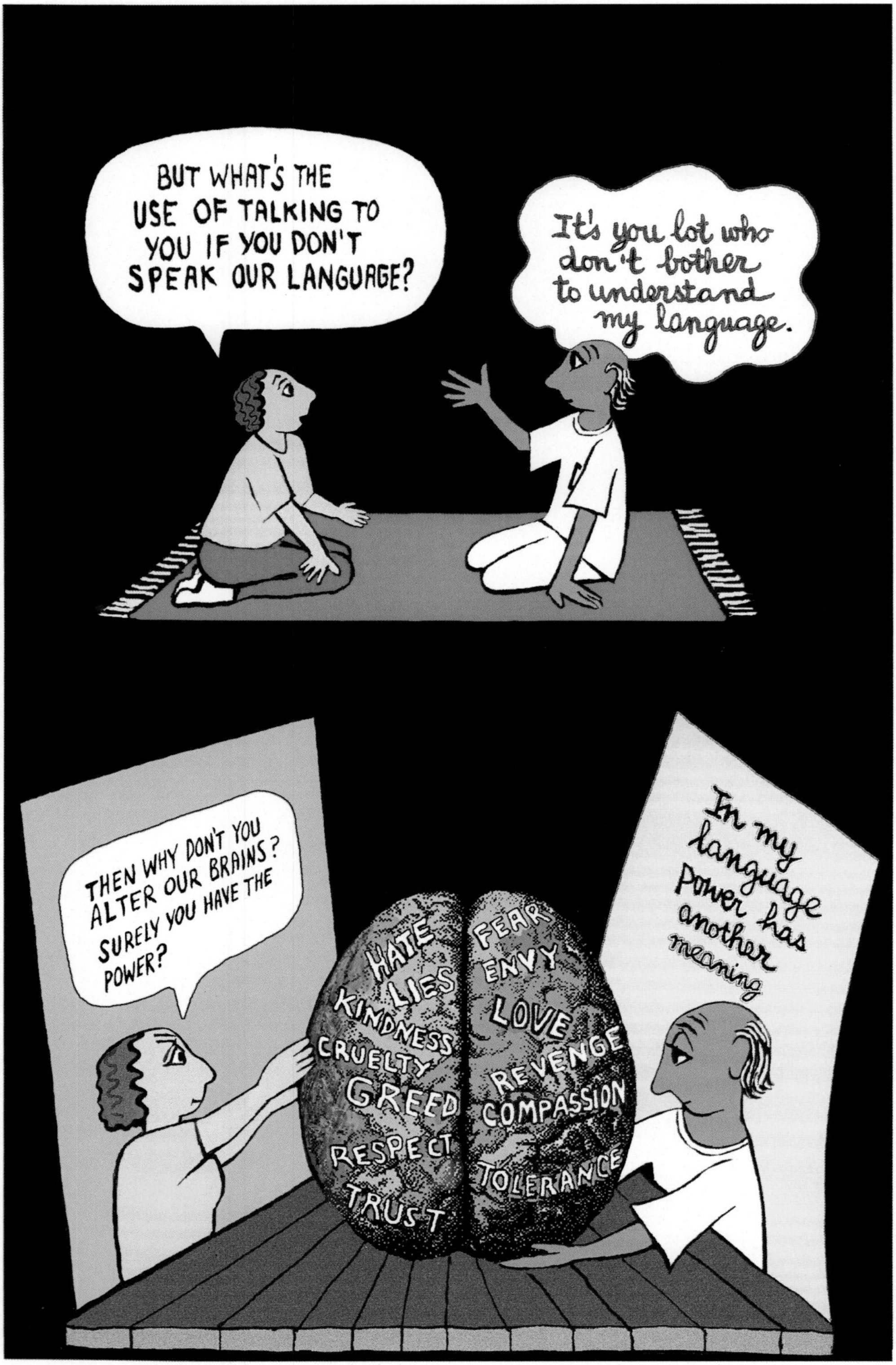
BUT WHAT'S THE USE OF TALKING TO YOU IF YOU DON'T SPEAK OUR LANGUAGE?
It's you lot who don't bother to understand my language.
THEN WHY DON'T YOU ALTER OUR BRAINS? SURELY YOU HAVE THE POWER?
In my language Power has another meaning
HATE
LIES
KINDNESS
CRUELTY
GREED
RESPECT
TRUST
FEAR
ENVY
LOVE
REVENGE
COMPASSION
TOLERANCE

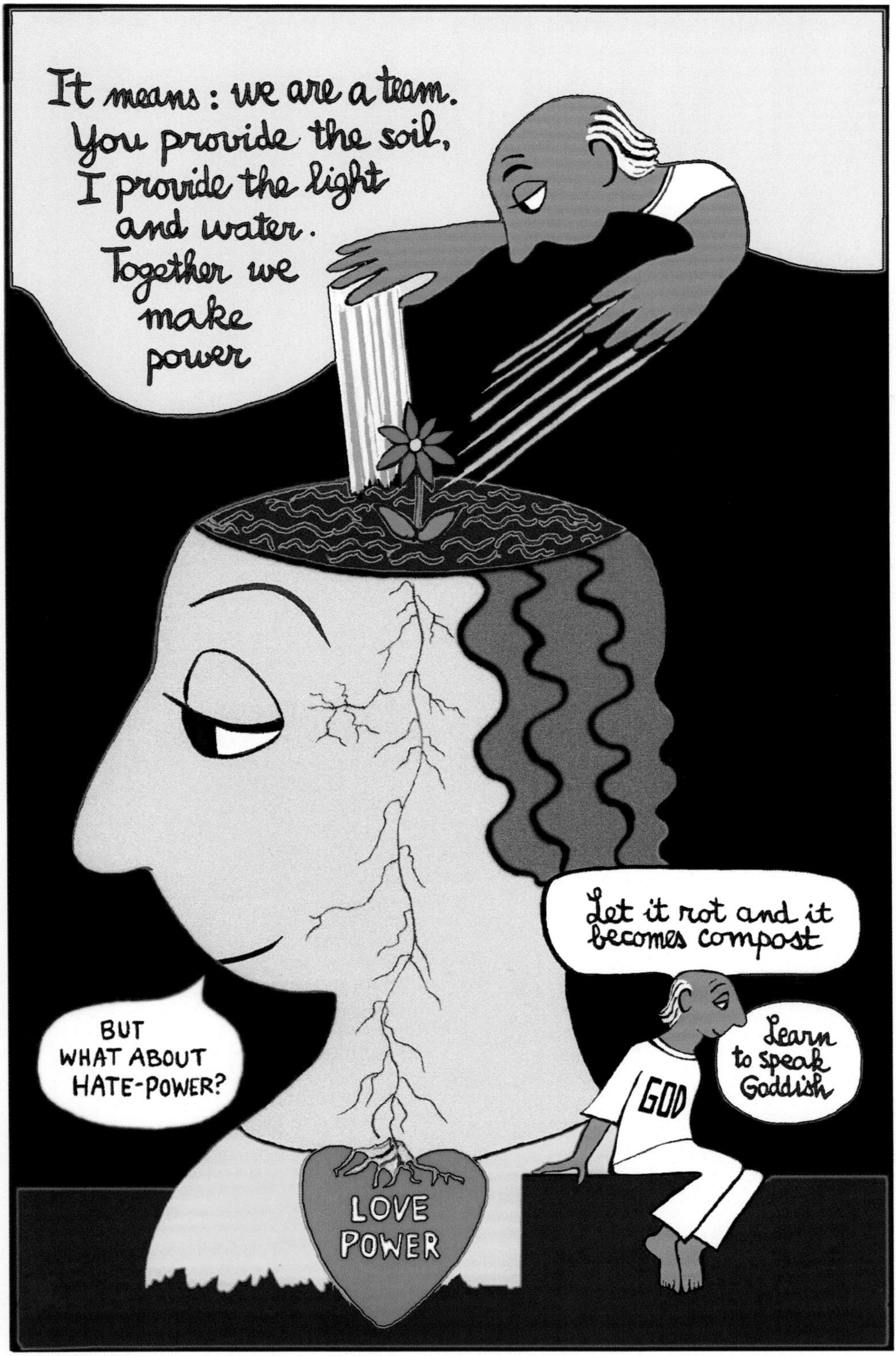
It means: we are a team. You provide the soil, I provide the light and water. Together we make power
LOVE POWER
Let it rot and it becomes compost
BUT WHAT ABOUT HATE-POWER?
GOD
Learn to speak Goddish

EIGHT

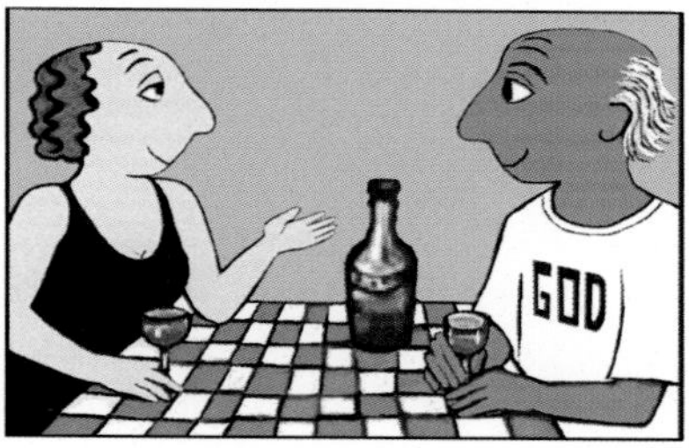
GOD

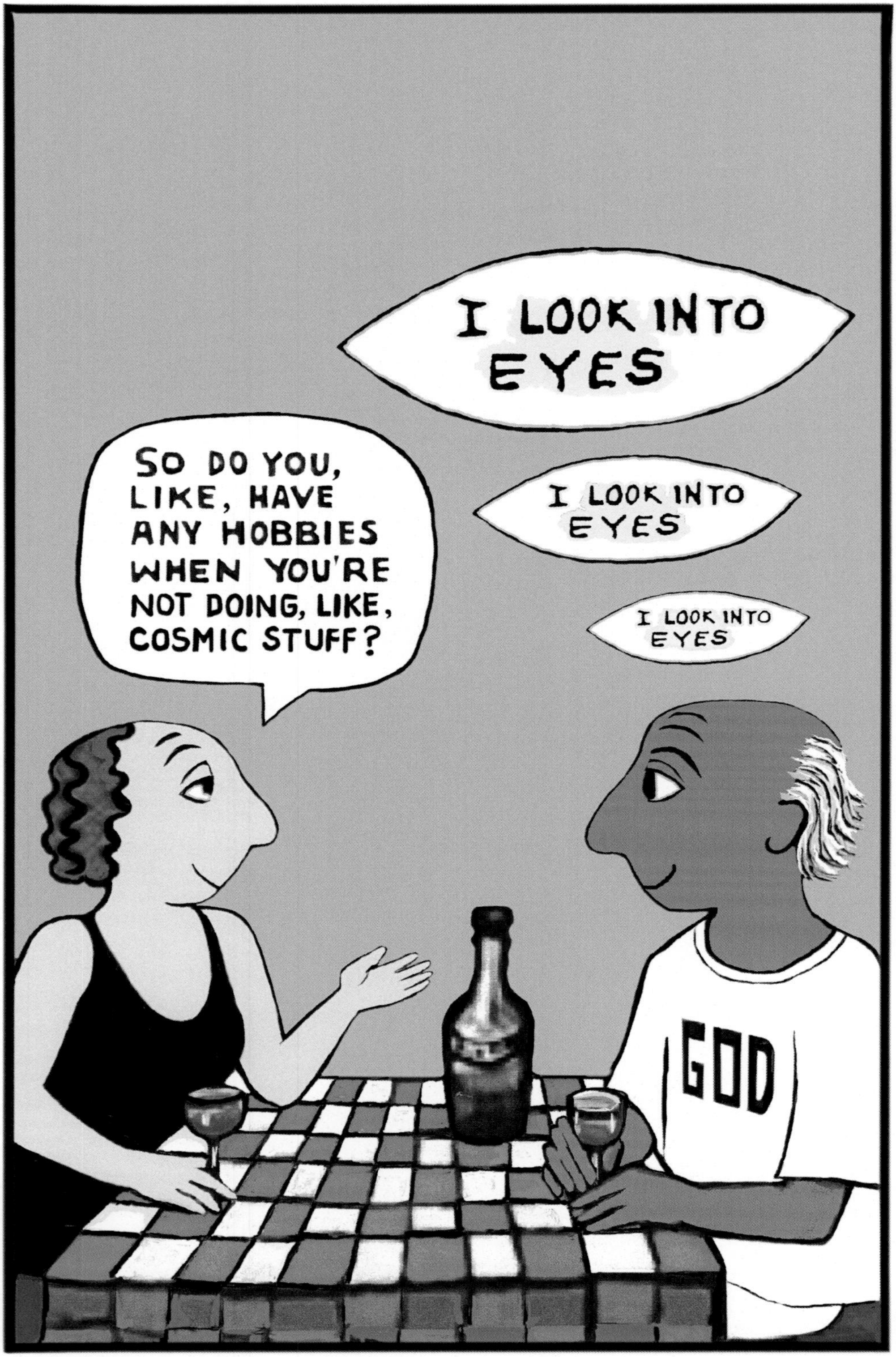
SO DO YOU, LIKE, HAVE ANY HOBBIES WHEN YOU'RE NOT DOING, LIKE, COSMIC STUFF?
I LOOK INTO EYES
I LOOK INTO EYES
I LOOK INTO EYES
GOD

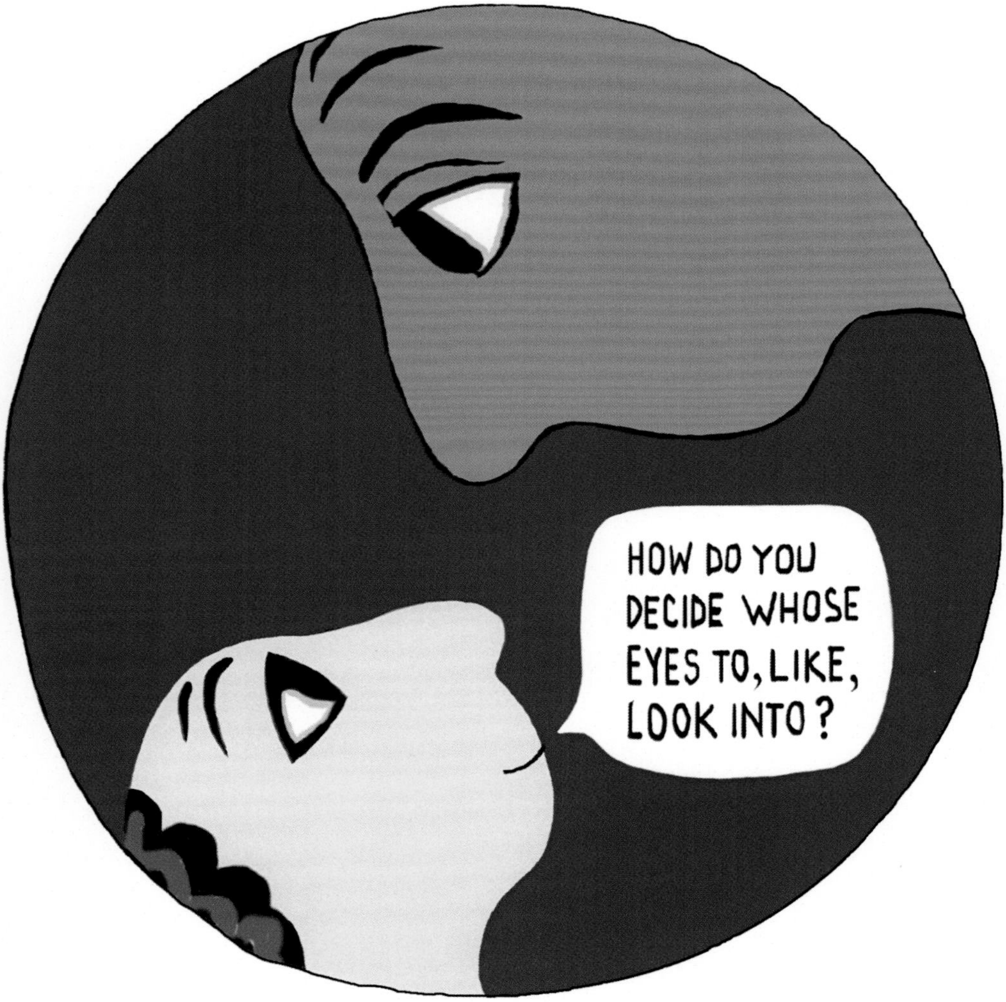
HOW DO YOU DECIDE WHOSE EYES TO, LIKE, LOOK INTO?

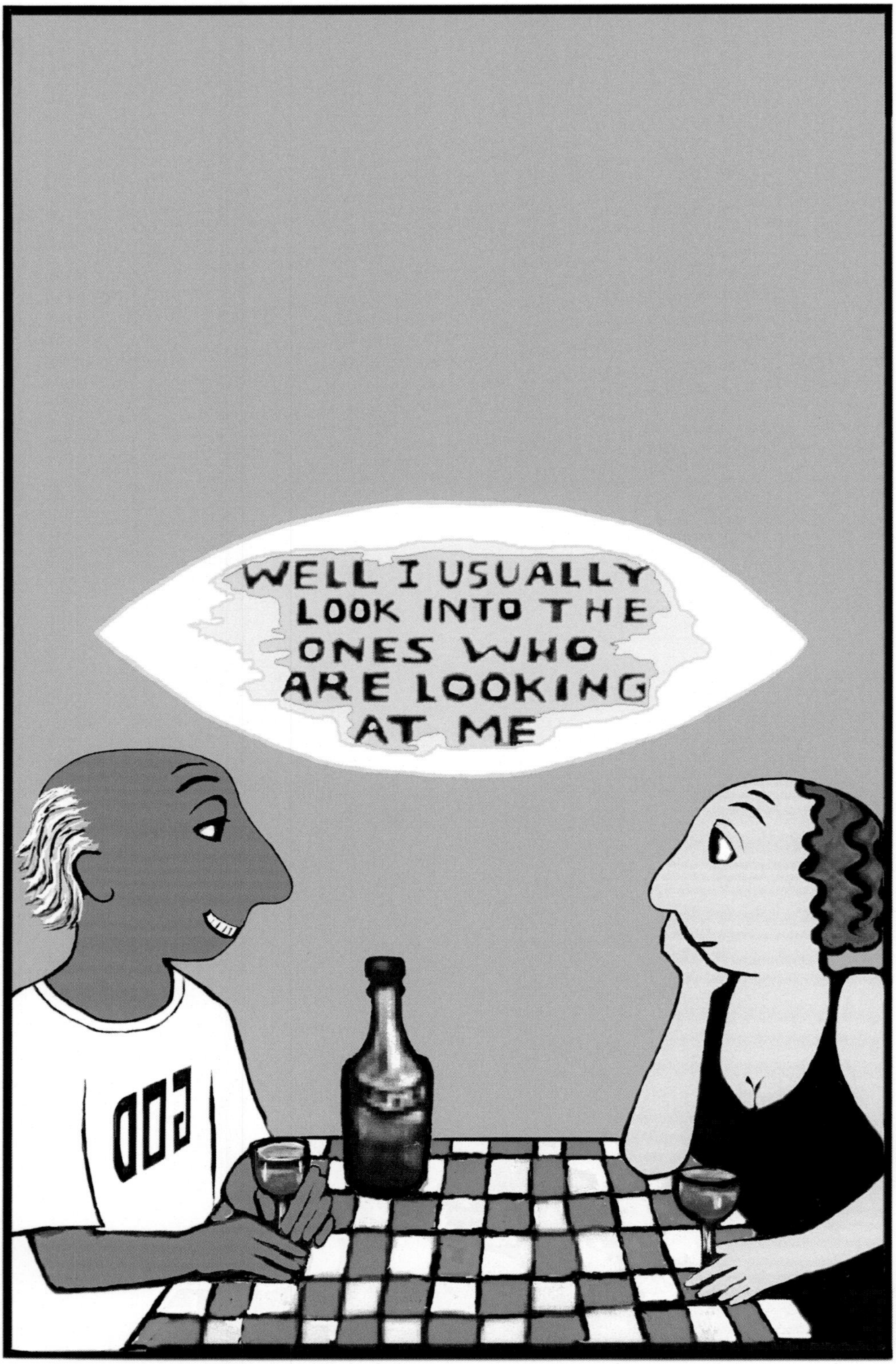
WELL I USUALLY LOOK INTO THE ONES WHO ARE LOOKING AT ME

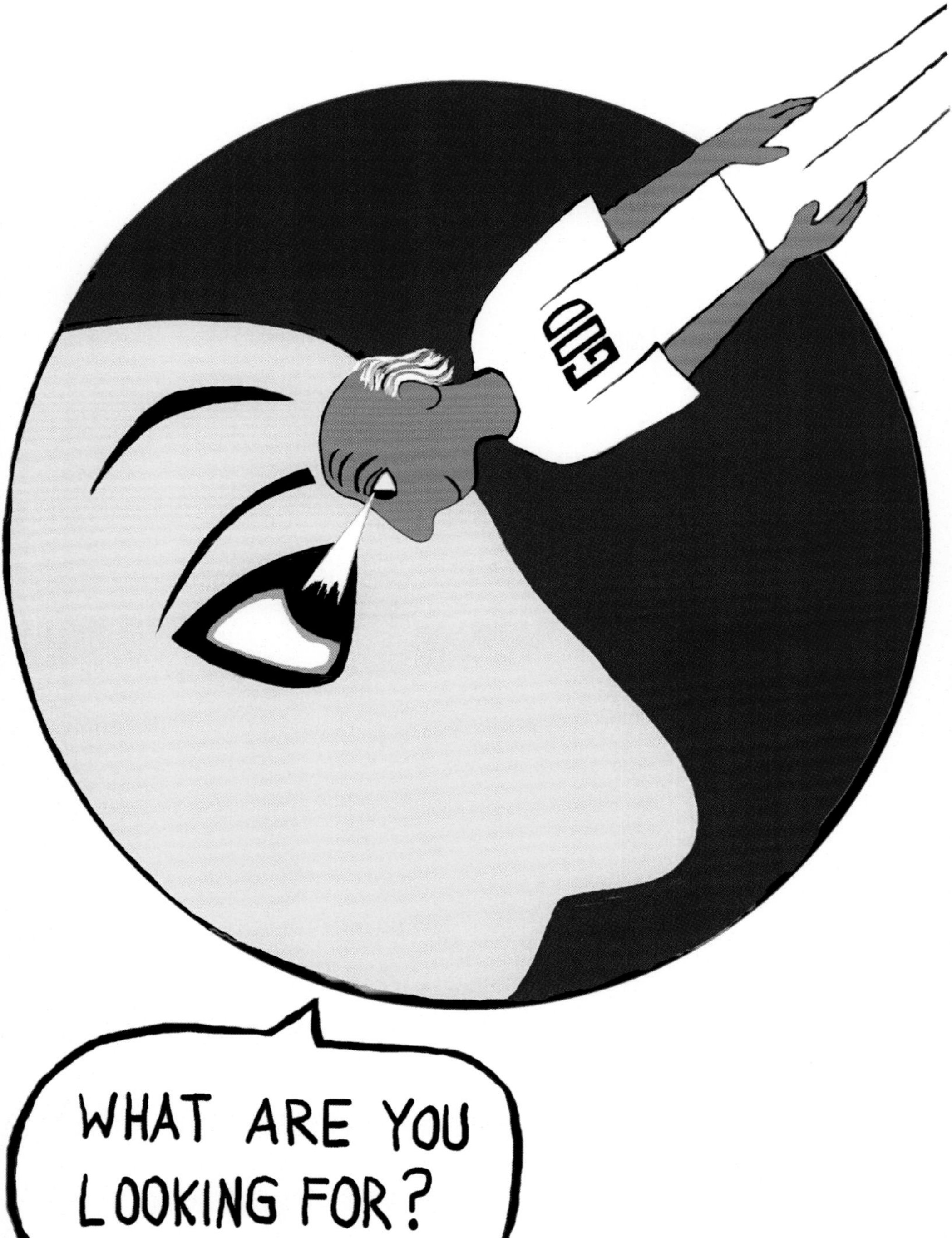
GOD
WHAT ARE YOU LOOKING FOR?

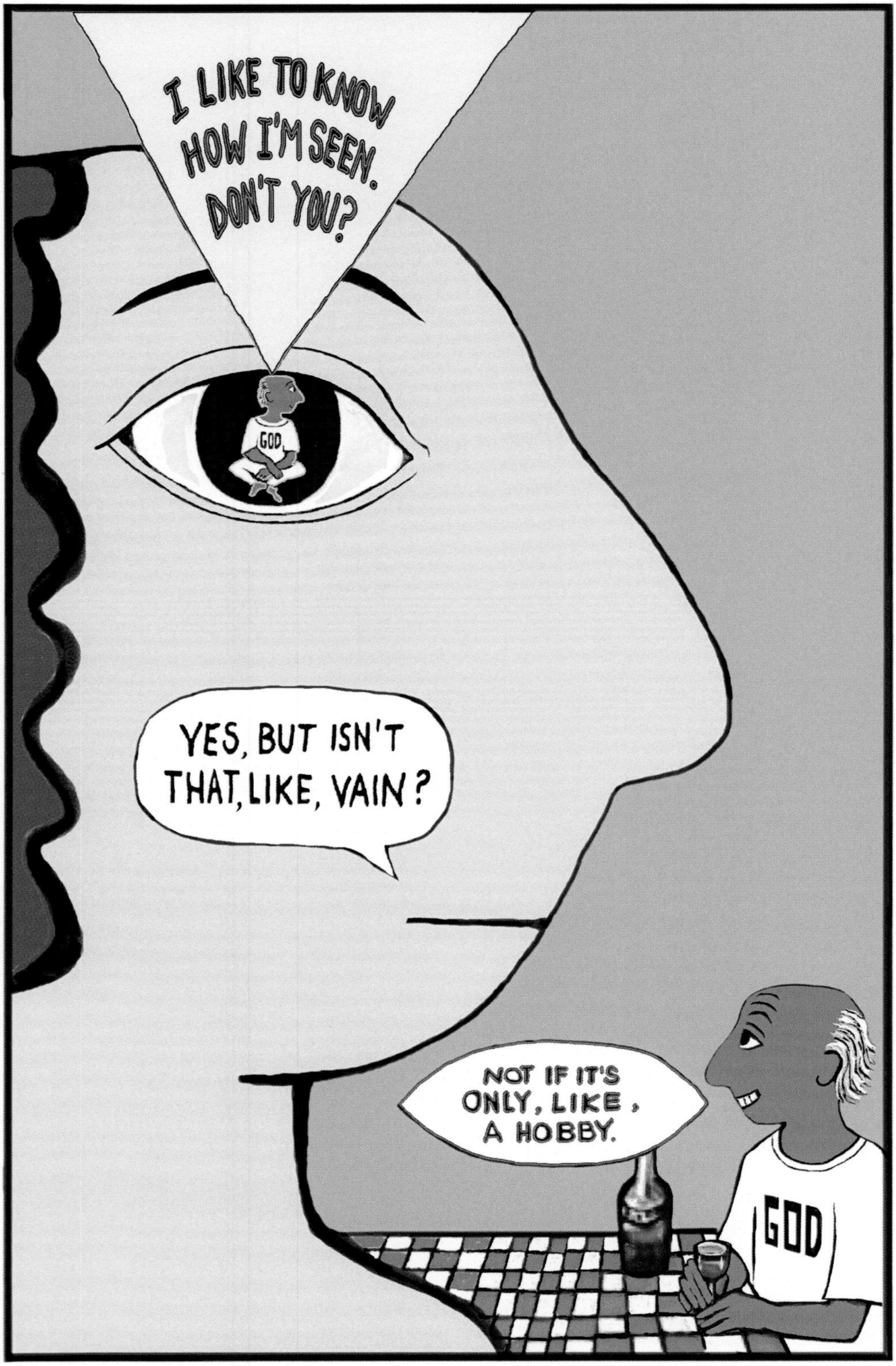
I LIKE TO KNOW HOW I'M SEEN. DON'T YOU?
GOD
YES, BUT ISN'T THAT, LIKE, VAIN?
NOT IF IT'S ONLY, LIKE, A HOBBY.
GOD

NINE

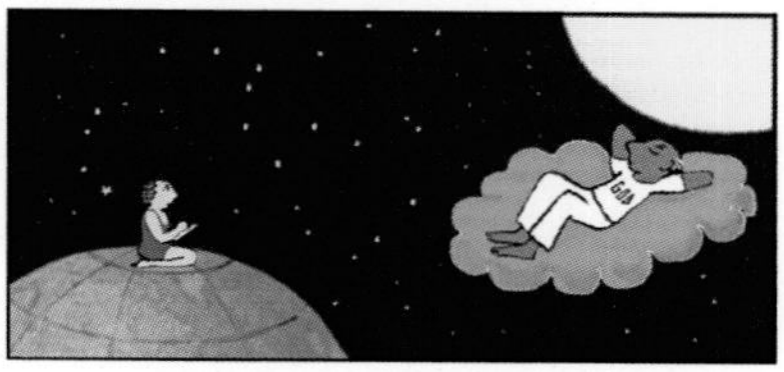

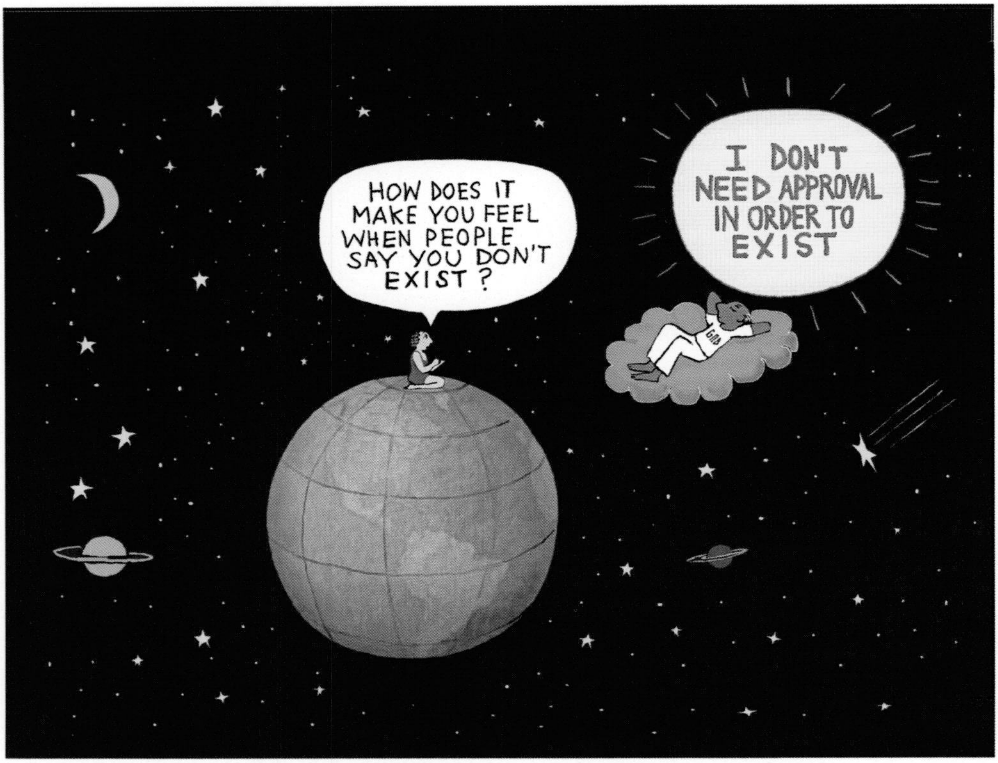
HOW DOES IT MAKE YOU FEEL WHEN PEOPLE SAY YOU DON'T EXIST?
I DON'T NEED APPROVAL IN ORDER TO EXIST

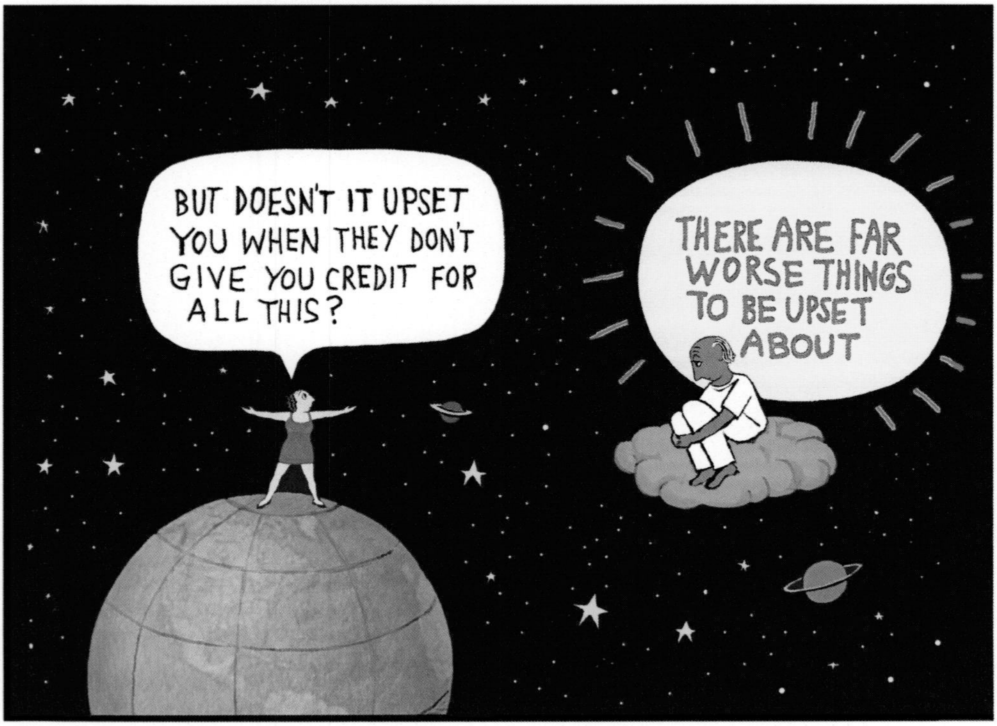
BUT DOESN'T IT UPSET YOU WHEN THEY DON'T GIVE YOU CREDIT FOR ALL THIS?
THERE ARE FAR WORSE THINGS TO BE UPSET ABOUT

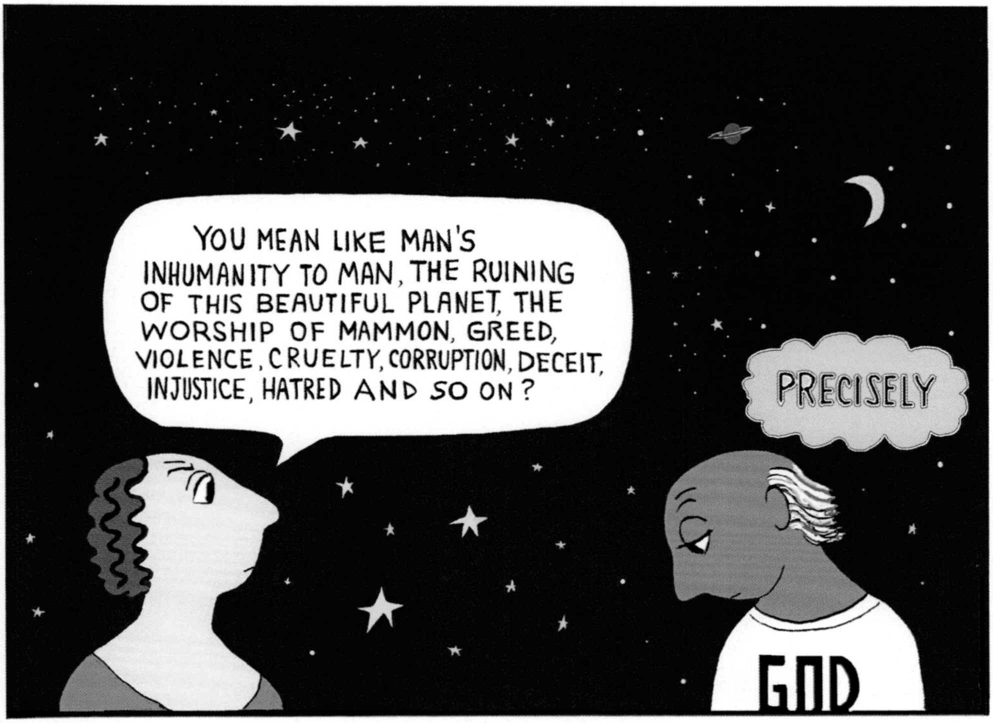
YOU MEAN LIKE MAN'S INHUMANITY TO MAN, THE RUINING OF THIS BEAUTIFUL PLANET, THE WORSHIP OF MAMMON, GREED, VIOLENCE, CRUELTY, CORRUPTION, DECEIT, INJUSTICE, HATRED AND SO ON?
PRECISELY
GOD

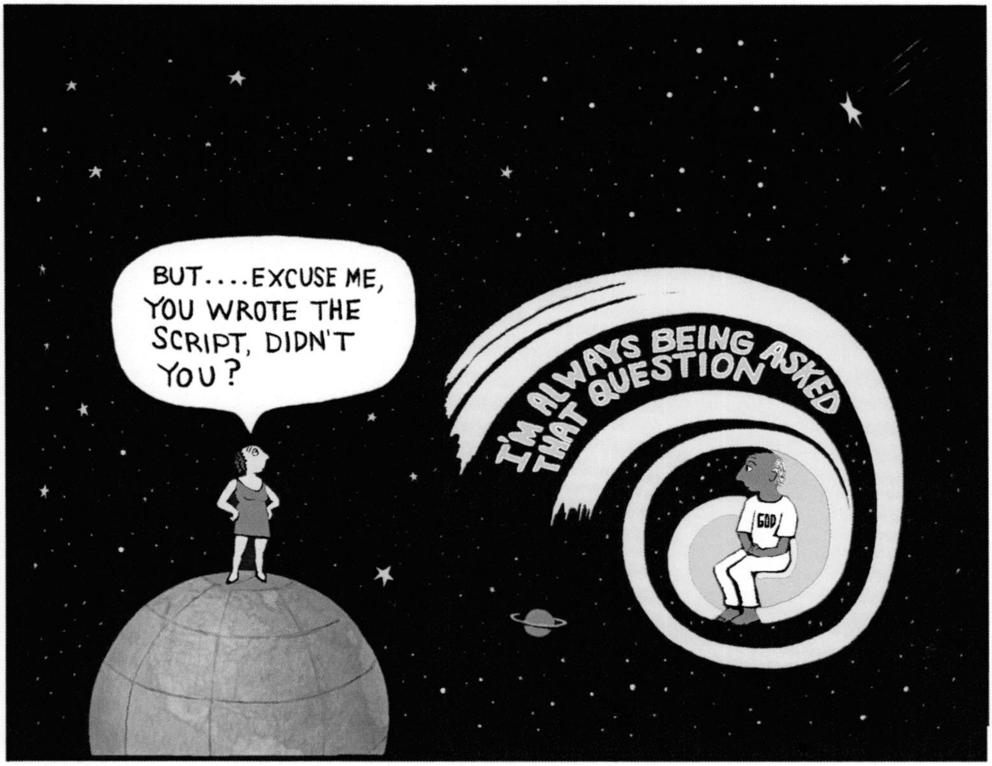
BUT....EXCUSE ME, YOU WROTE THE SCRIPT, DIDN'T YOU?
I'M ALWAYS BEING ASKED THAT QUESTION
GOD

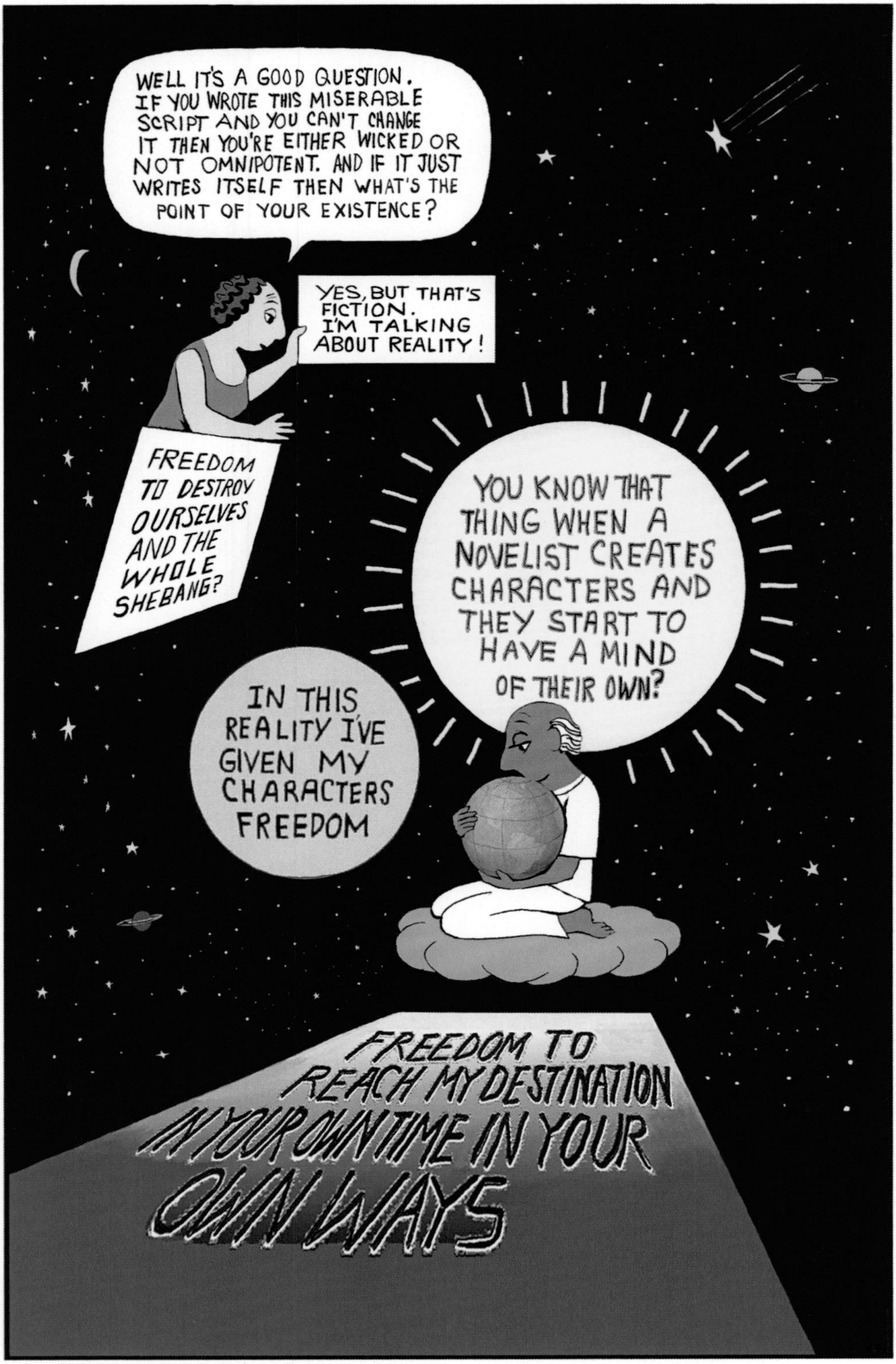

WELL IT'S A GOOD QUESTION. IF YOU WROTE THIS MISERABLE SCRIPT AND YOU CAN'T CHANGE IT THEN YOU'RE EITHER WICKED OR NOT OMNIPOTENT. AND IF IT JUST WRITES ITSELF THEN WHAT'S THE POINT OF YOUR EXISTENCE?
YES, BUT THAT'S FICTION. I'M TALKING ABOUT REALITY!
YOU KNOW THAT THING WHEN A NOVELIST CREATES CHARACTERS AND THEY START TO HAVE A MIND OF THEIR OWN?
IN THIS REALITY I'VE GIVEN MY CHARACTERS FREEDOM
FREEDOM TO DESTROY OURSELVES AND THE WHOLE SHEBANG?
FREEDOM TO REACH MY DESTINATION IN YOUR OWN TIME IN YOUR OWN WAYS

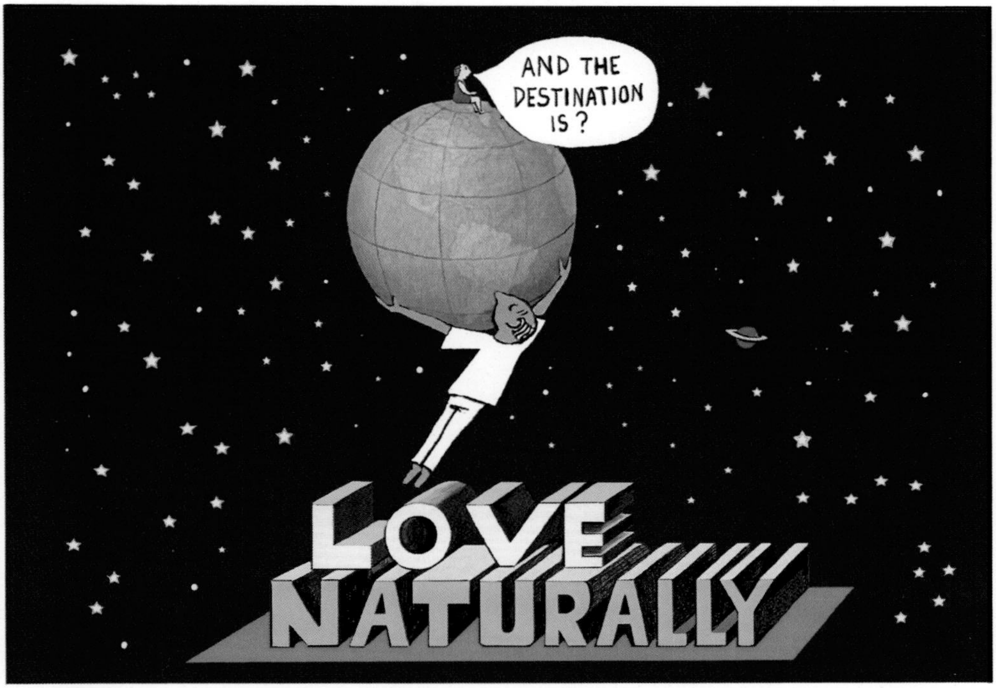
AND THE DESTINATION IS?
LOVE NATURALLY

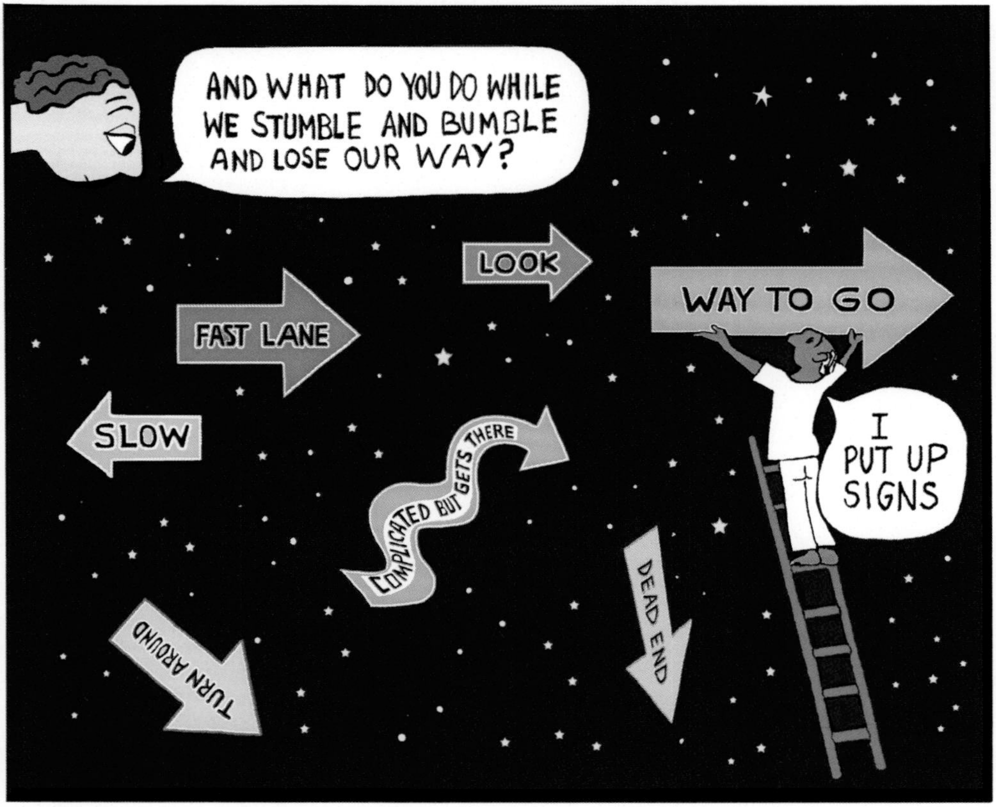
AND WHAT DO YOU DO WHILE WE STUMBLE AND BUMBLE AND LOSE OUR WAY?
LOOK
WAY TO GO
FAST LANE
SLOW
COMPLICATED BUT GETS THERE
I PUT UP SIGNS
DEAD END
TURN AROUND

TEN

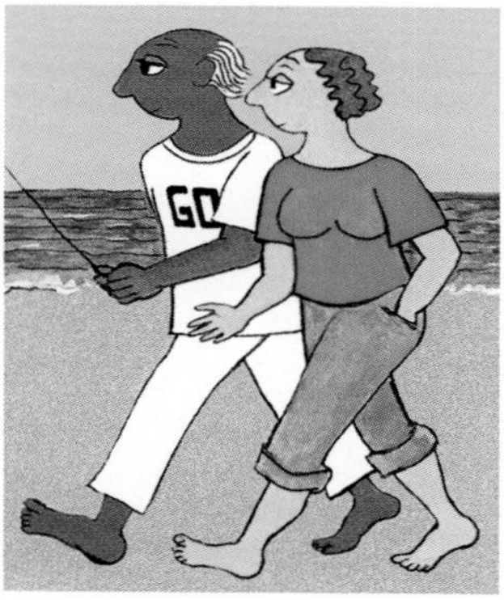
GO

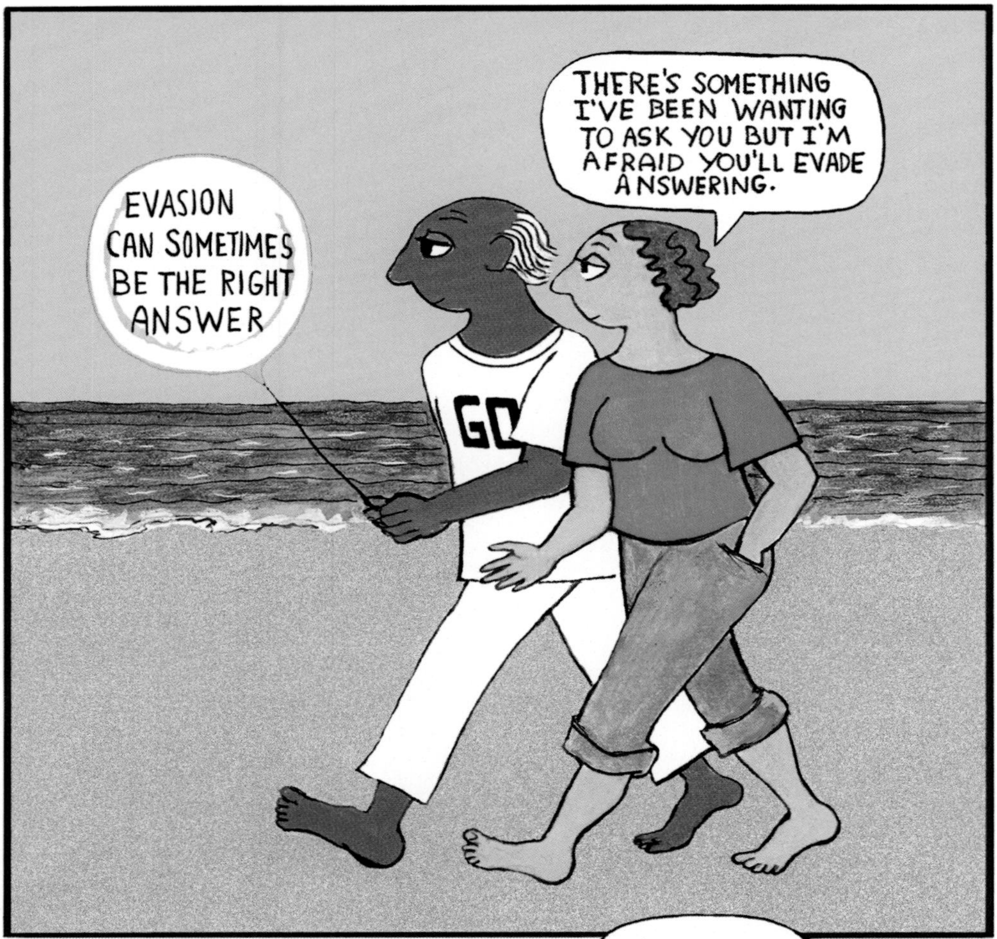
THERE'S SOMETHING I'VE BEEN WANTING TO ASK YOU BUT I'M AFRAID YOU'LL EVADE ANSWERING.
EVASION CAN SOMETIMES BE THE RIGHT ANSWER
GO

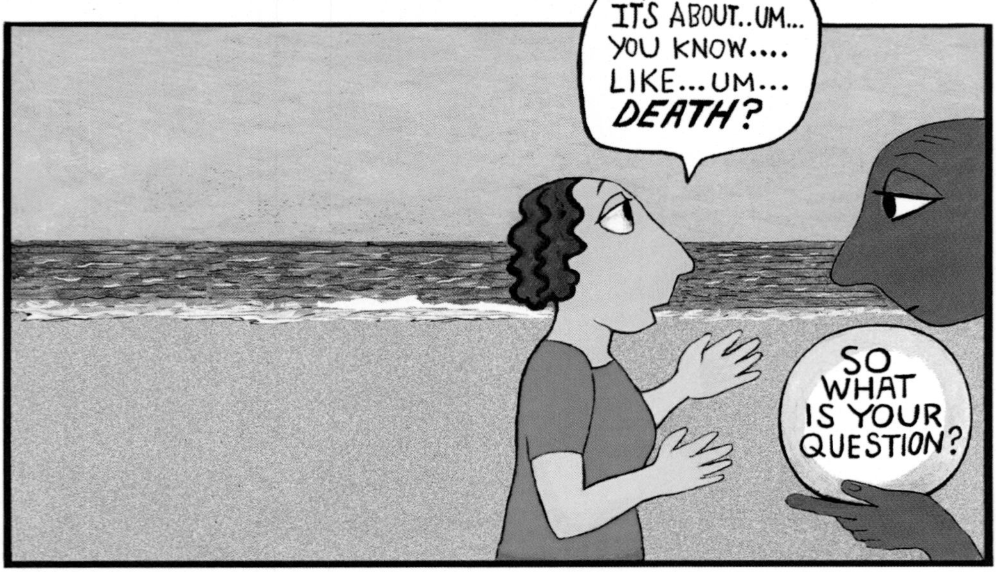
IT'S ABOUT..UM... YOU KNOW.... LIKE...UM... *DEATH*?
SO WHAT IS YOUR QUESTION?

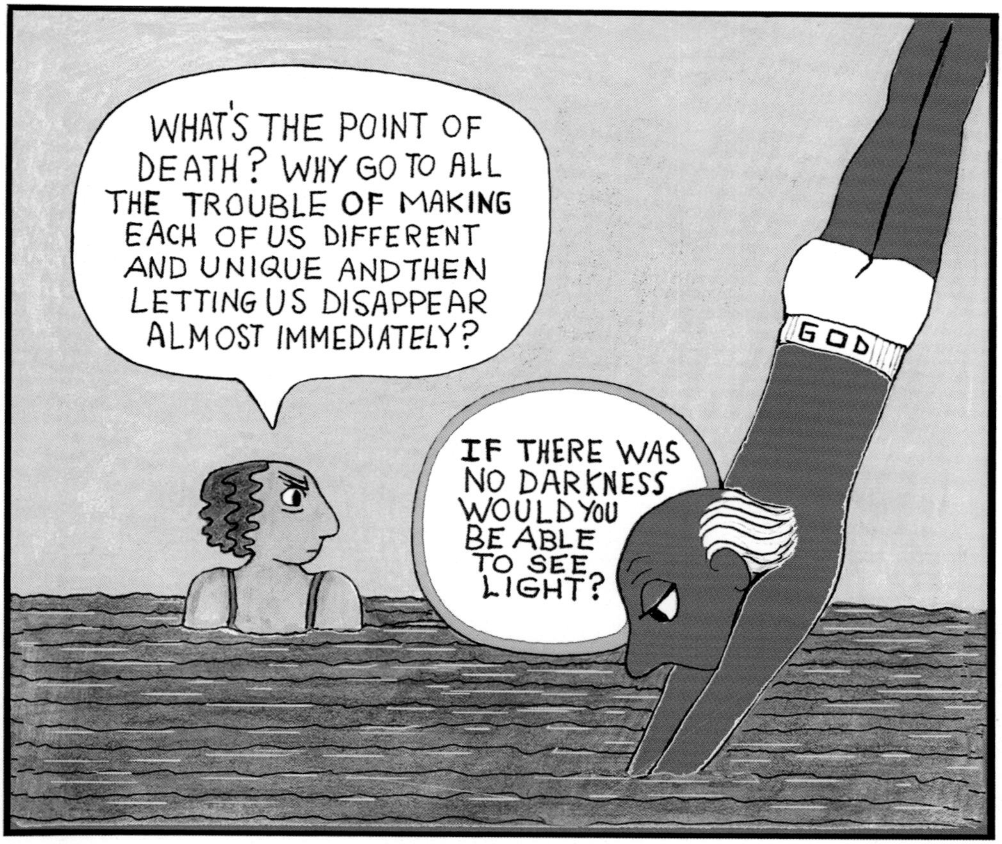
WHAT'S THE POINT OF DEATH? WHY GO TO ALL THE TROUBLE OF MAKING EACH OF US DIFFERENT AND UNIQUE AND THEN LETTING US DISAPPEAR ALMOST IMMEDIATELY?
GOD
IF THERE WAS NO DARKNESS WOULD YOU BE ABLE TO SEE LIGHT?

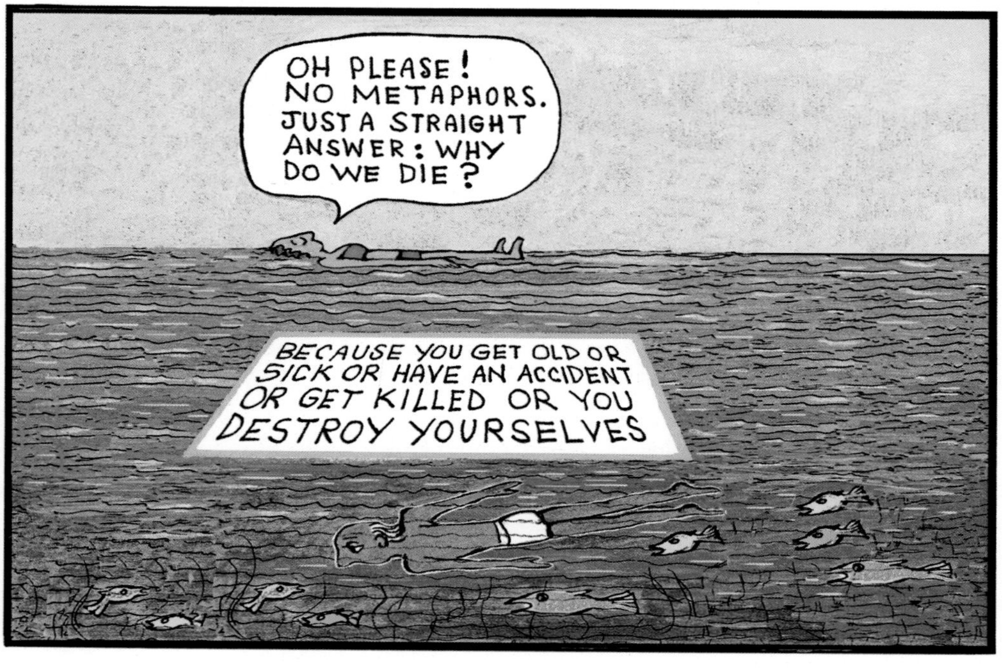
OH PLEASE! NO METAPHORS. JUST A STRAIGHT ANSWER: WHY DO WE DIE?
BECAUSE YOU GET OLD OR SICK OR HAVE AN ACCIDENT OR GET KILLED OR YOU DESTROY YOURSELVES

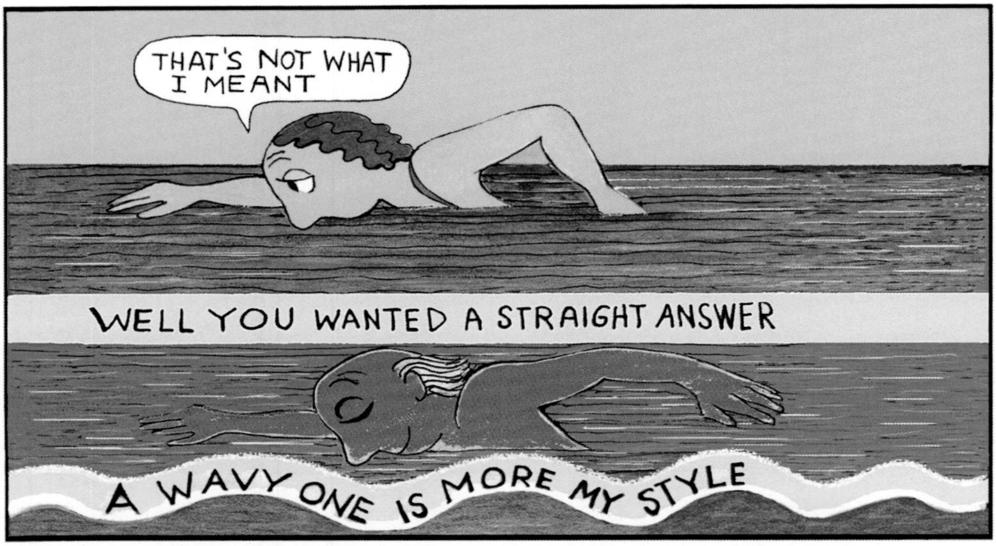
THAT'S NOT WHAT I MEANT
WELL YOU WANTED A STRAIGHT ANSWER
A WAVY ONE IS MORE MY STYLE

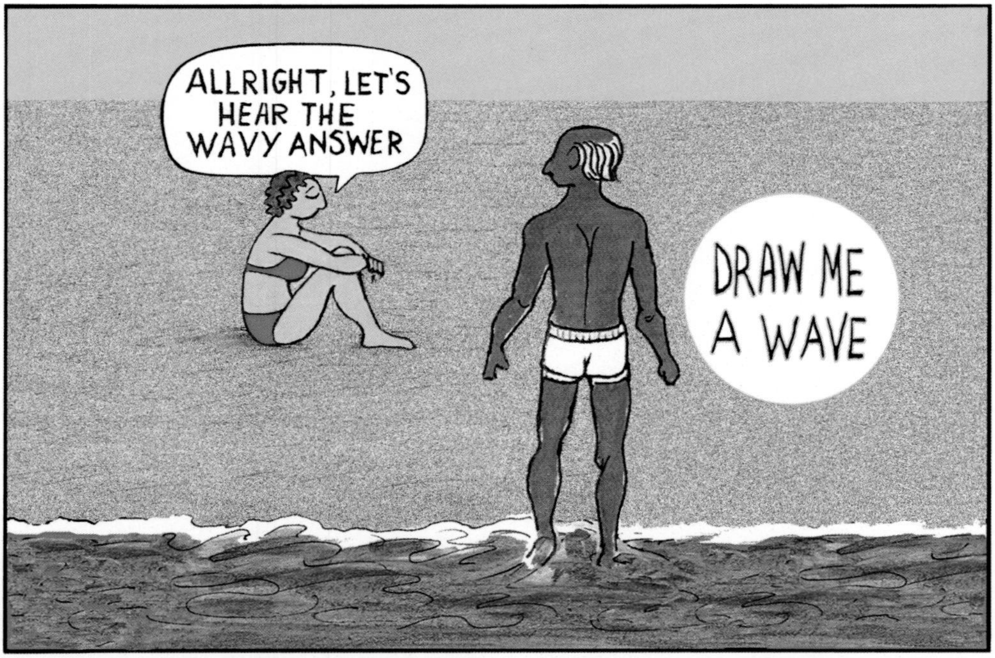
ALLRIGHT, LET'S HEAR THE WAVY ANSWER
DRAW ME A WAVE

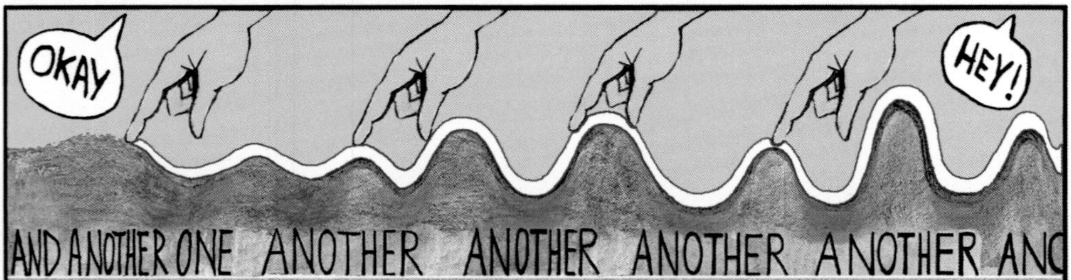
OKAY
HEY!
AND ANOTHER ONE ANOTHER ANOTHER ANOTHER ANOTHER ANC

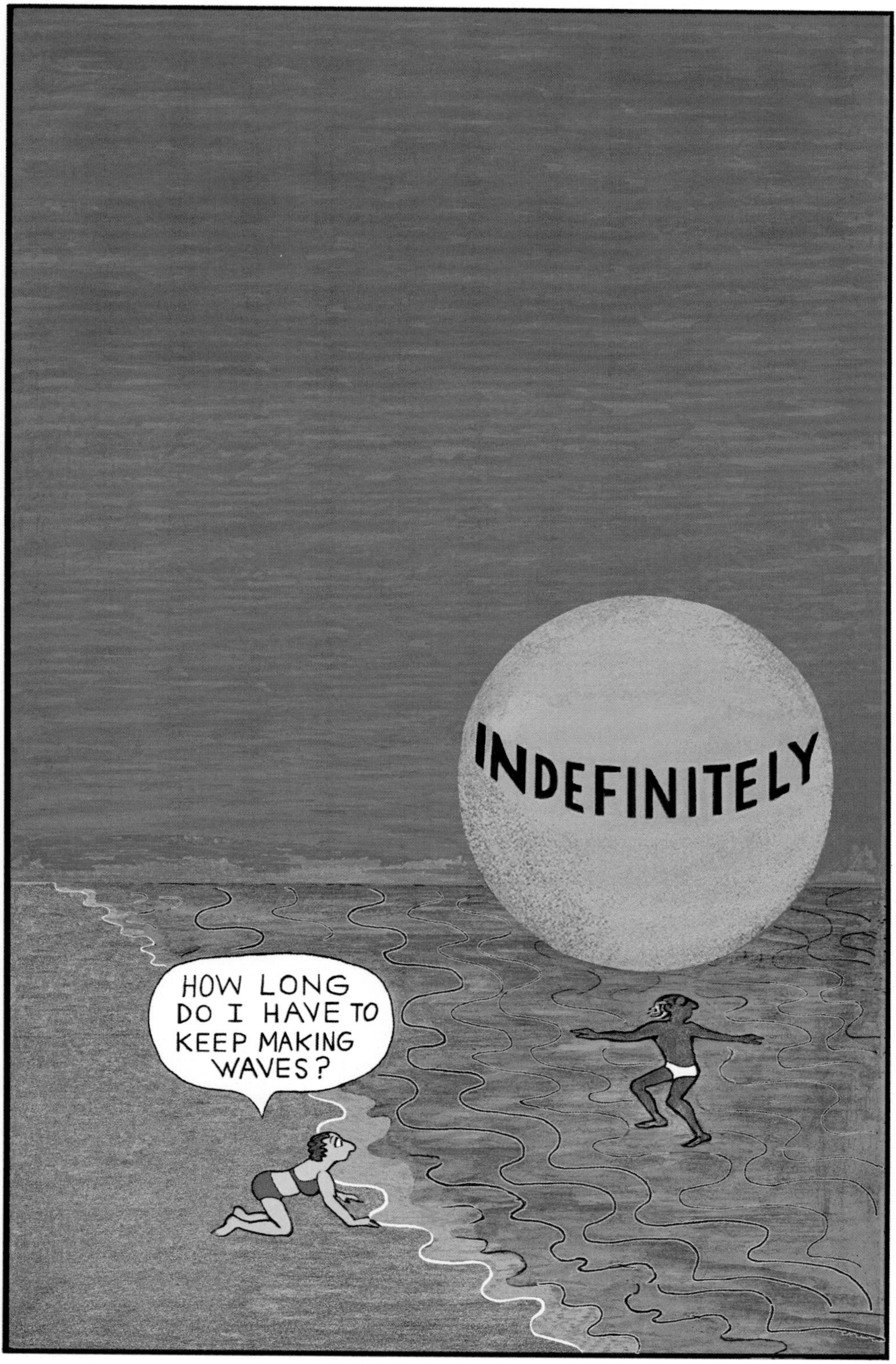
INDEFINITELY
HOW LONG DO I HAVE TO KEEP MAKING WAVES?

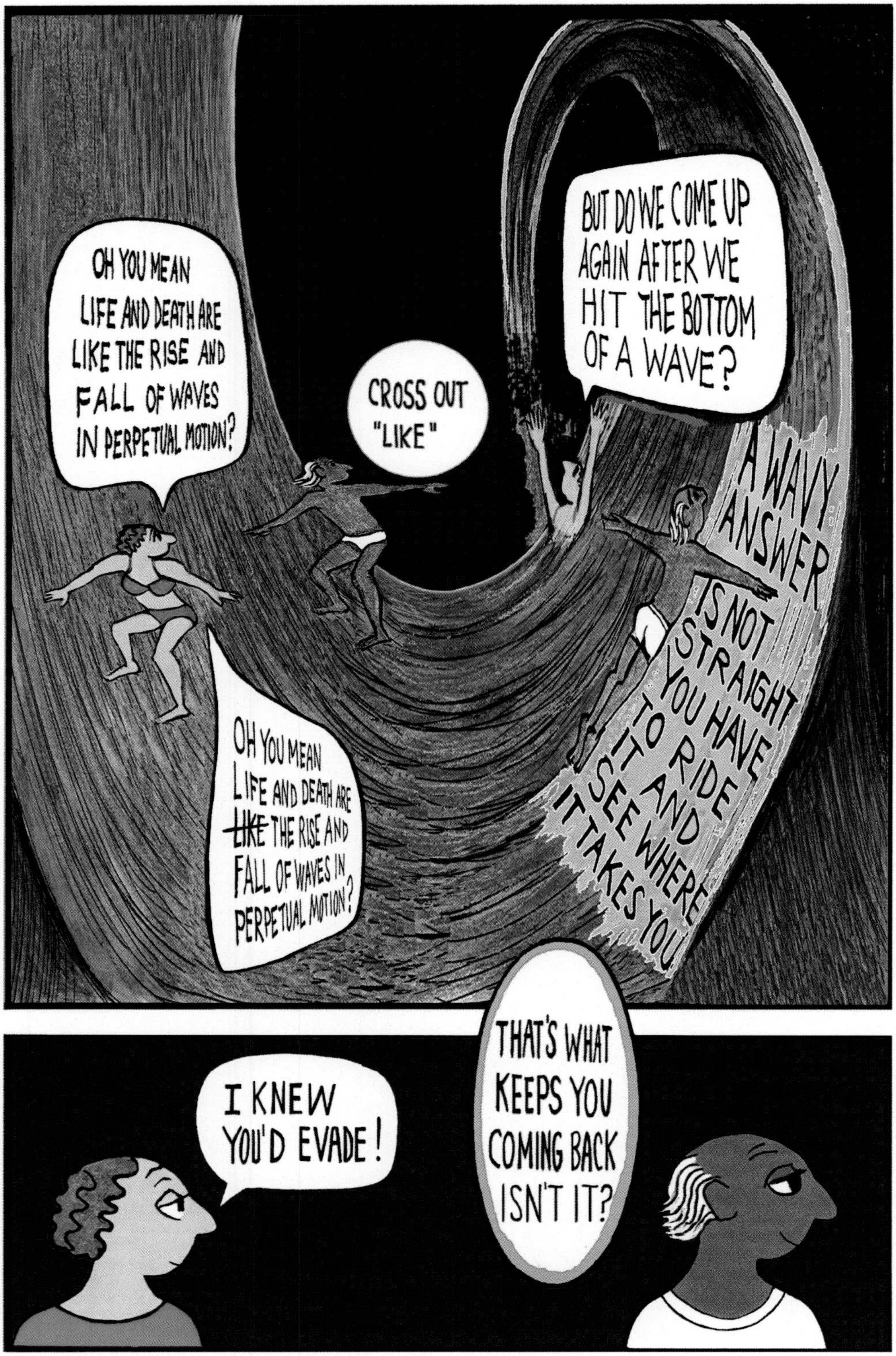
OH YOU MEAN LIFE AND DEATH ARE LIKE THE RISE AND FALL OF WAVES IN PERPETUAL MOTION?
CROSS OUT "LIKE"
BUT DO WE COME UP AGAIN AFTER WE HIT THE BOTTOM OF A WAVE?
OH YOU MEAN LIFE AND DEATH ARE ~~LIKE~~ THE RISE AND FALL OF WAVES IN PERPETUAL MOTION?
A WAVY ANSWER IS NOT STRAIGHT YOU HAVE TO RIDE IT AND SEE WHERE IT TAKES YOU
I KNEW YOU'D EVADE!
THAT'S WHAT KEEPS YOU COMING BACK ISN'T IT?

ELEVEN

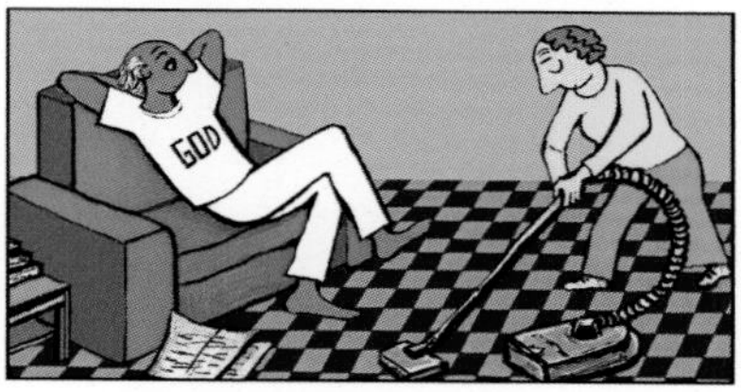
GOD

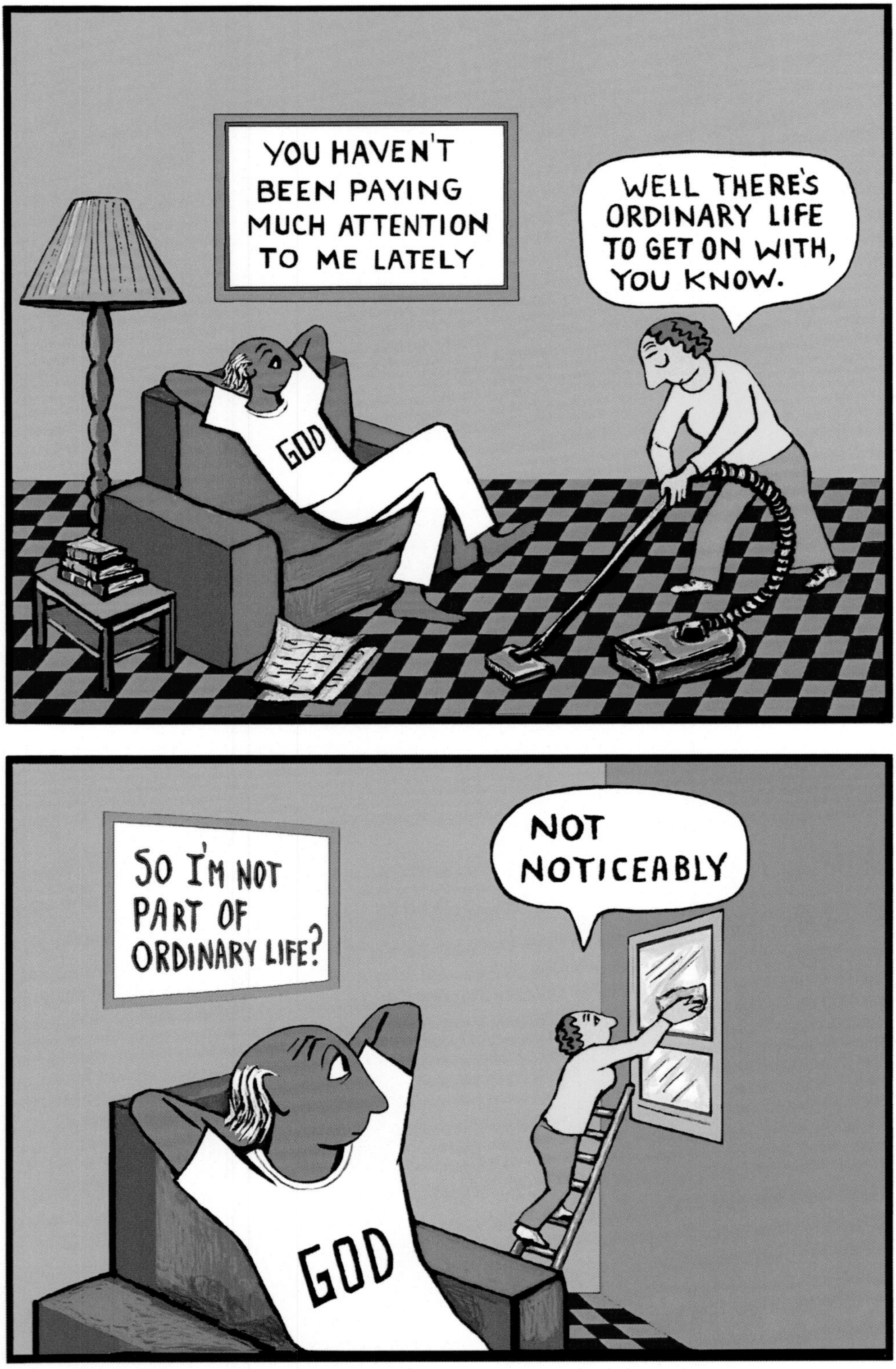
YOU HAVEN'T BEEN PAYING MUCH ATTENTION TO ME LATELY
WELL THERE'S ORDINARY LIFE TO GET ON WITH, YOU KNOW.
GOD
SO I'M NOT PART OF ORDINARY LIFE?
NOT NOTICEABLY
GOD

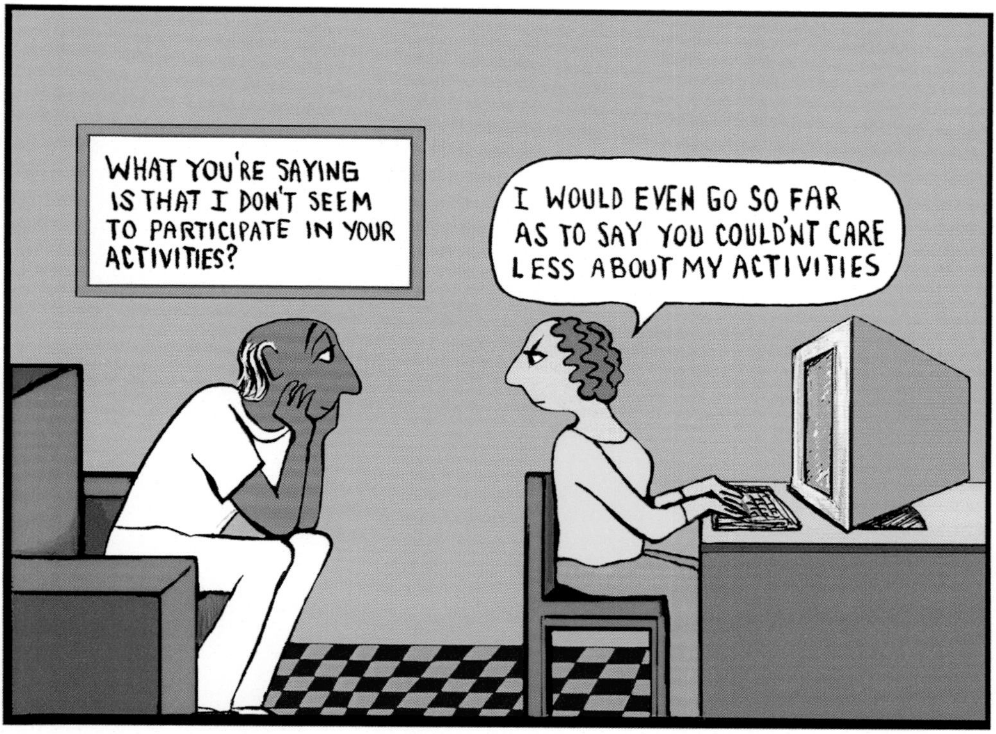
WHAT YOU'RE SAYING IS THAT I DON'T SEEM TO PARTICIPATE IN YOUR ACTIVITIES?
I WOULD EVEN GO SO FAR AS TO SAY YOU COULDN'T CARE LESS ABOUT MY ACTIVITIES

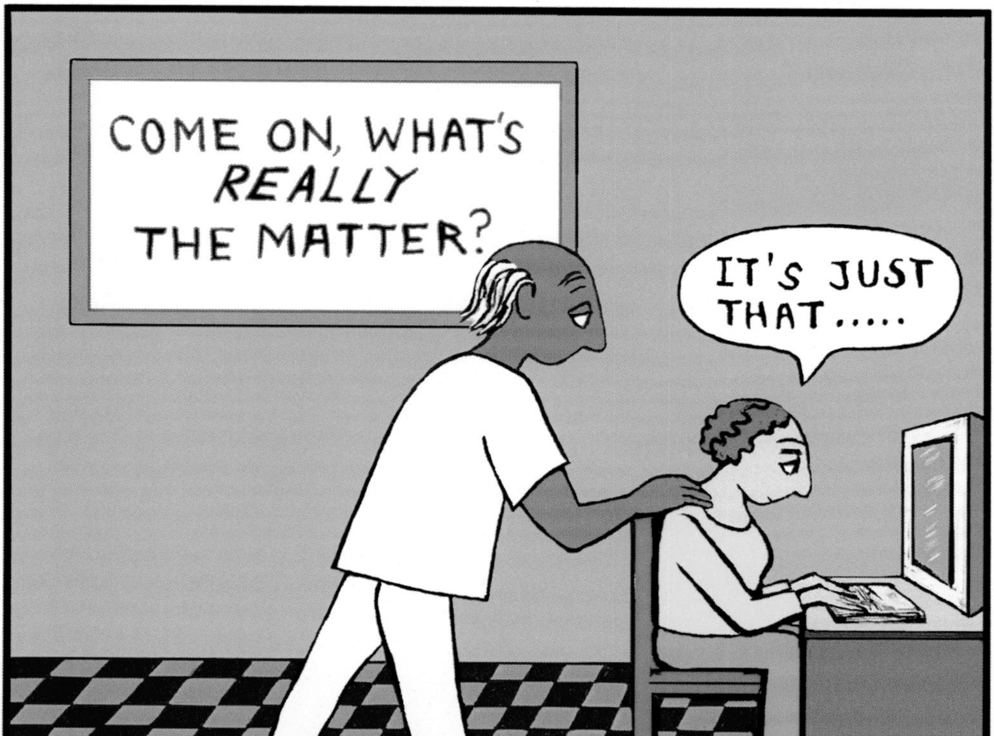
COME ON, WHAT'S *REALLY* THE MATTER?
IT'S JUST THAT.....

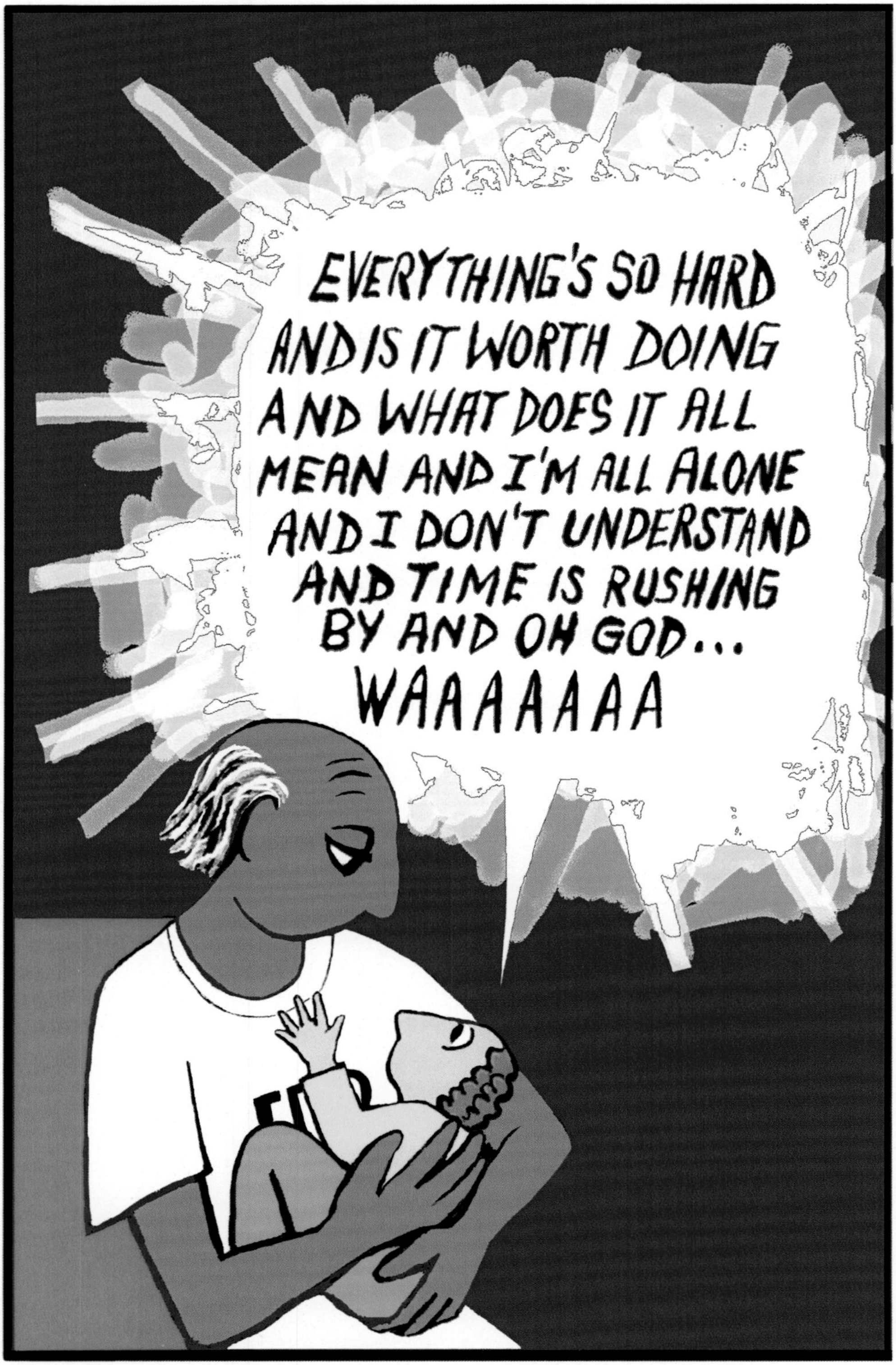
EVERYTHING'S SO HARD AND IS IT WORTH DOING AND WHAT DOES IT ALL MEAN AND I'M ALL ALONE AND I DON'T UNDERSTAND AND TIME IS RUSHING BY AND OH GOD...
WAAAAAAA

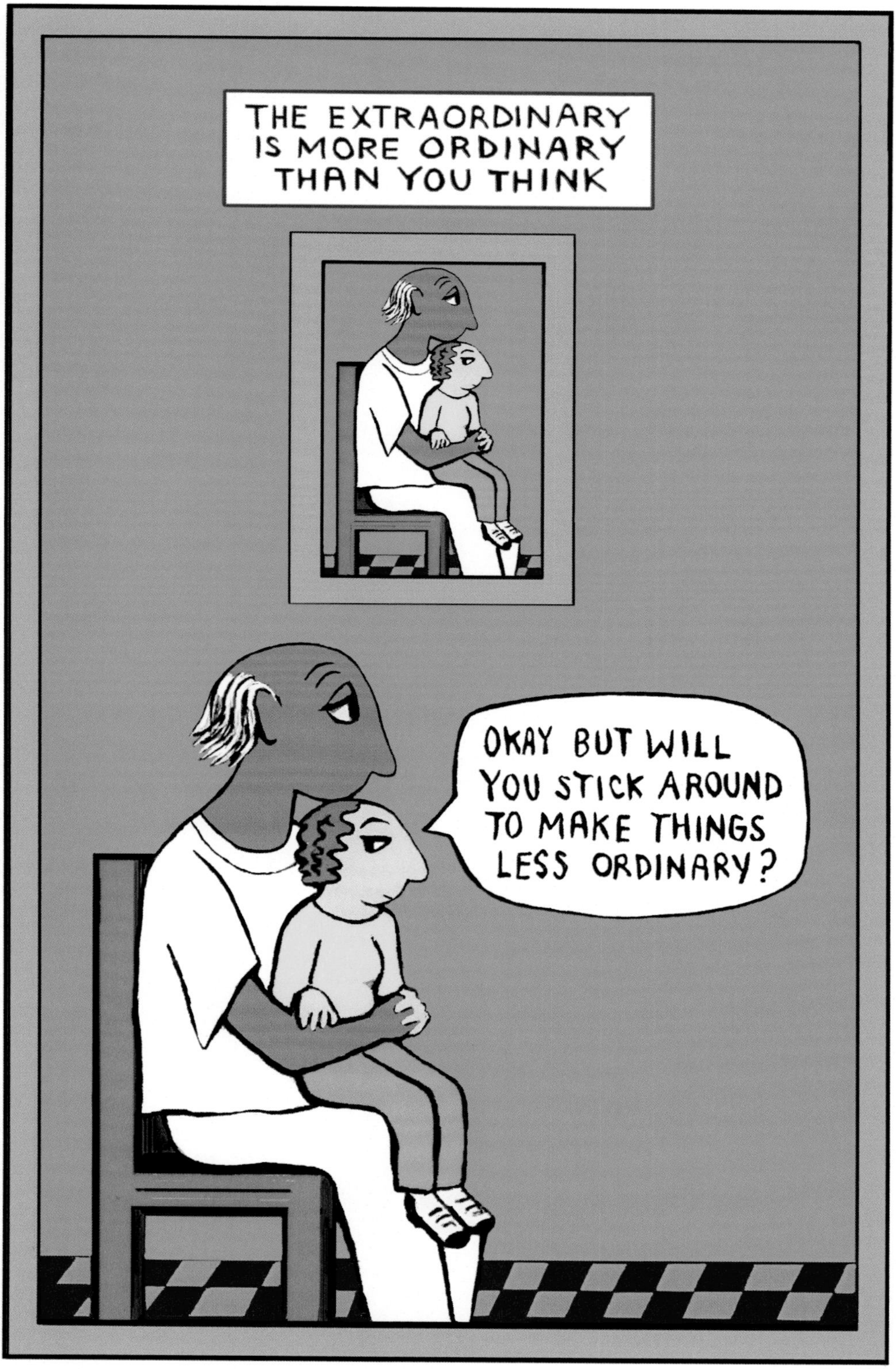
THE EXTRAORDINARY IS MORE ORDINARY THAN YOU THINK
OKAY BUT WILL YOU STICK AROUND TO MAKE THINGS LESS ORDINARY?

TWELVE

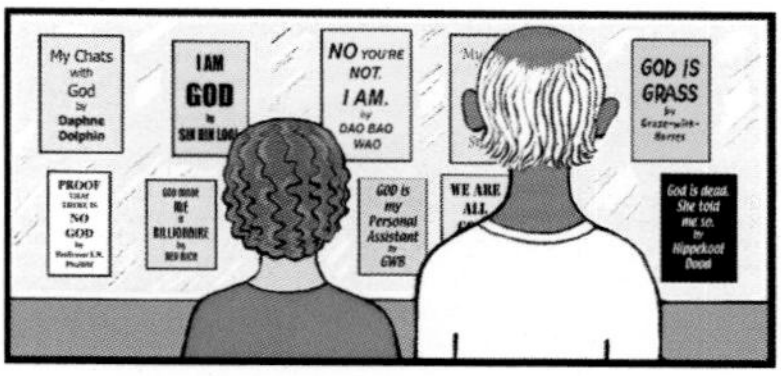
My Chats with God by Daphne Dolphin
I AM GOD by
NO YOU'RE NOT. I AM. by DAO BAO WAO
GOD IS GRASS by
PROOF
NO GOD
GOD is my Personal Assistant by GWB
WE ARE ALL
God is dead. She told me so. by Hippekoot Dood

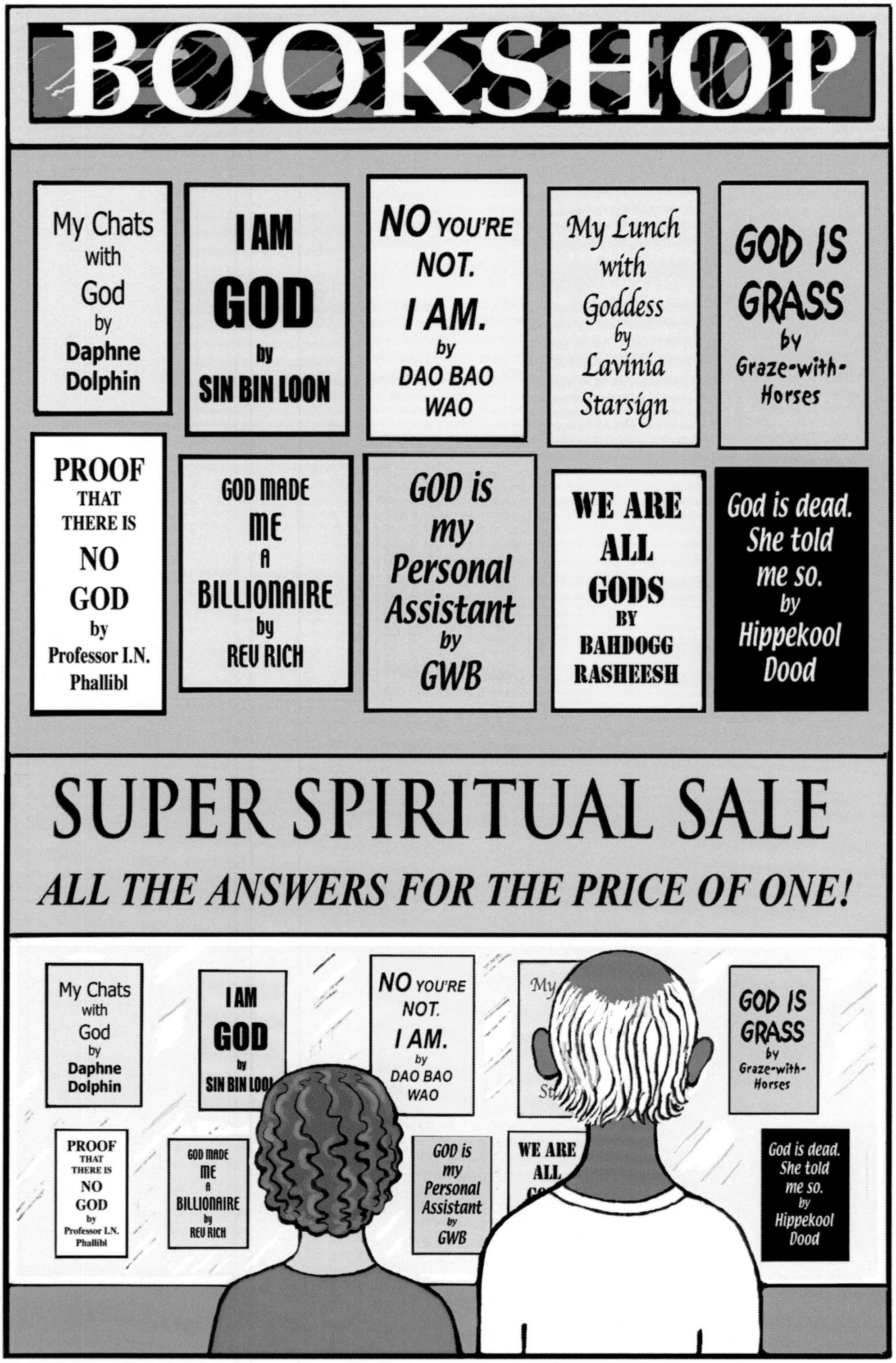
BOOKSHOP
My Chats with God by Daphne Dolphin
I AM GOD by SIN BIN LOON
NO YOU'RE NOT. I AM. by DAO BAO WAO
My Lunch with Goddess by Lavinia Starsign
GOD IS GRASS by Graze-with-Horses
PROOF THAT THERE IS NO GOD by Professor I.N. Phallibl
GOD MADE ME A BILLIONAIRE by REV RICH
GOD is my Personal Assistant by GWB
WE ARE ALL GODS BY BAHDOGG RASHEESH
God is dead. She told me so. by Hippekool Dood
SUPER SPIRITUAL SALE
ALL THE ANSWERS FOR THE PRICE OF ONE!

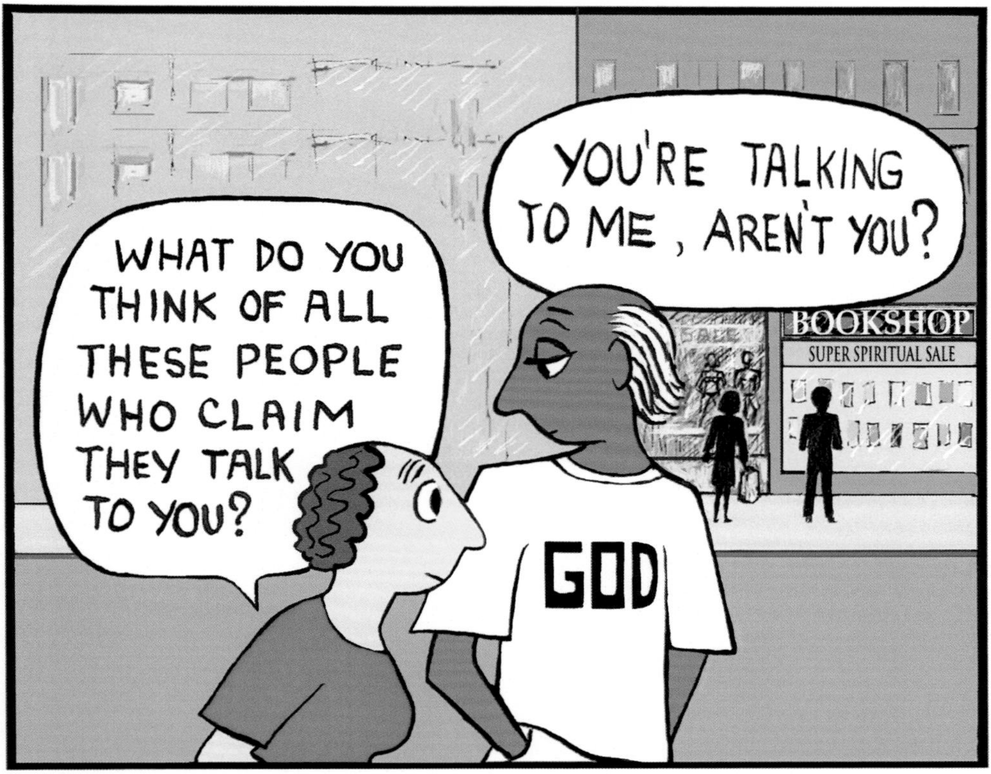
WHAT DO YOU THINK OF ALL THESE PEOPLE WHO CLAIM THEY TALK TO YOU?
YOU'RE TALKING TO ME, AREN'T YOU?
BOOKSHOP
SUPER SPIRITUAL SALE
GOD

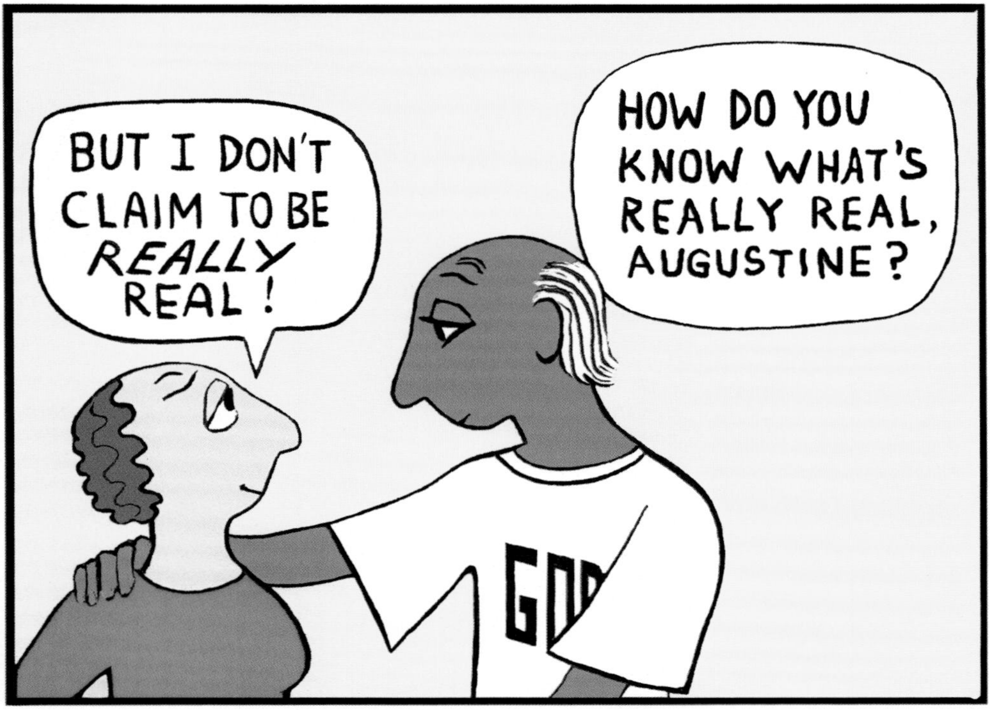
BUT I DON'T CLAIM TO BE *REALLY* REAL!
HOW DO YOU KNOW WHAT'S REALLY REAL, AUGUSTINE?

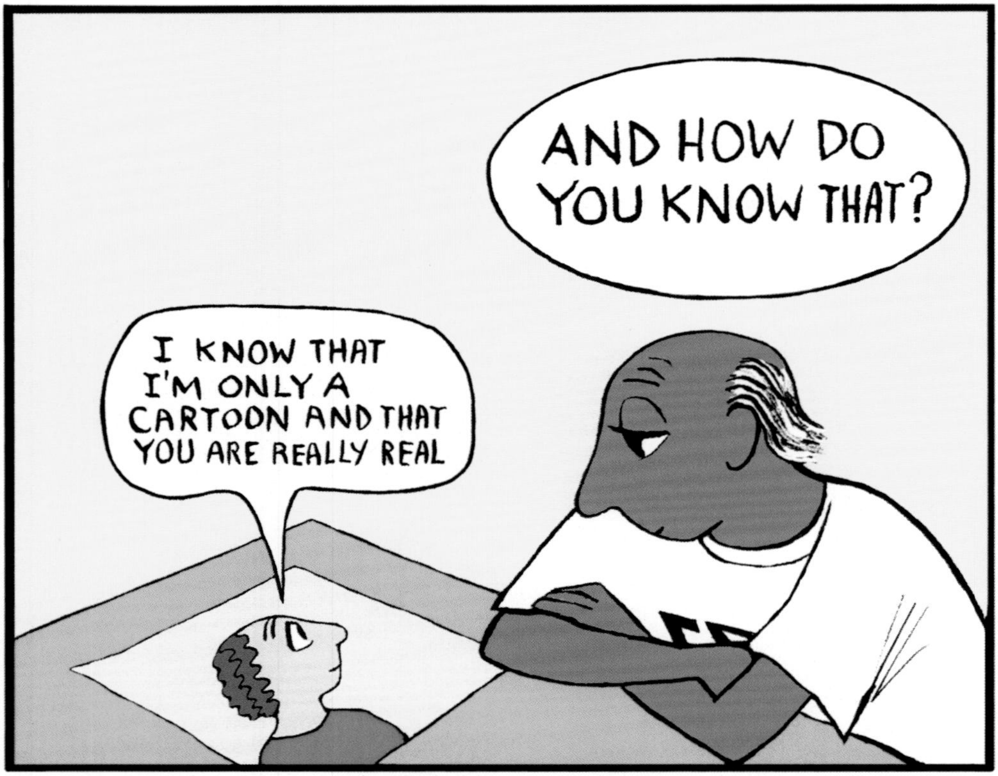
AND HOW DO YOU KNOW THAT?
I KNOW THAT I'M ONLY A CARTOON AND THAT YOU ARE REALLY REAL

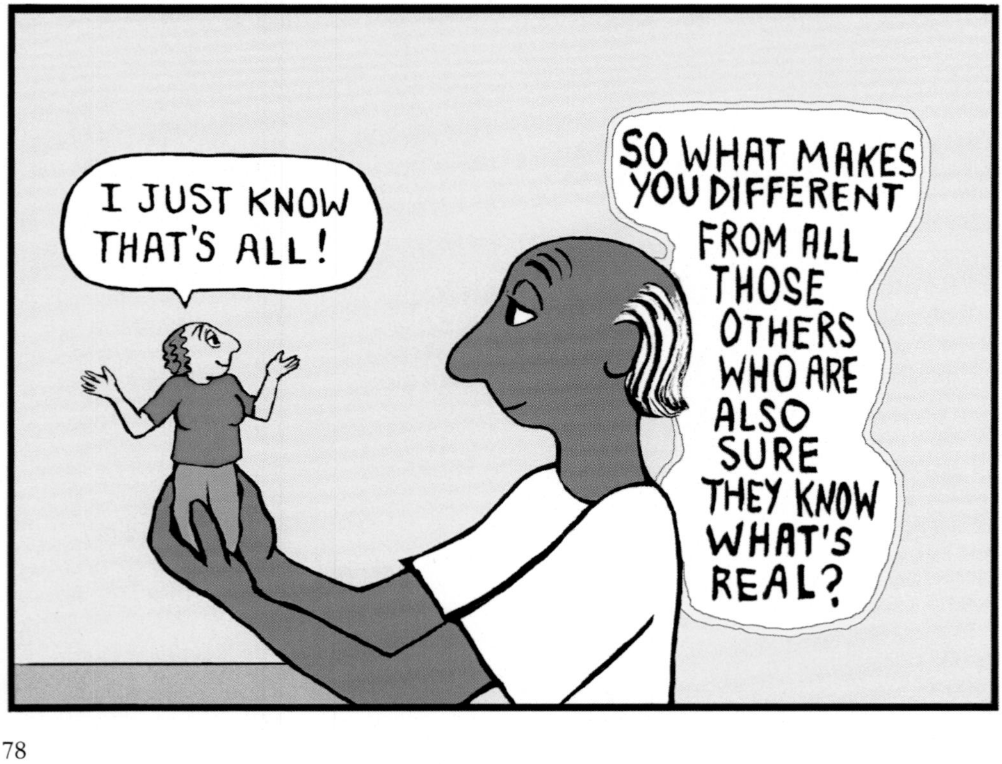
I JUST KNOW THAT'S ALL!
SO WHAT MAKES YOU DIFFERENT FROM ALL THOSE OTHERS WHO ARE ALSO SURE THEY KNOW WHAT'S REAL?

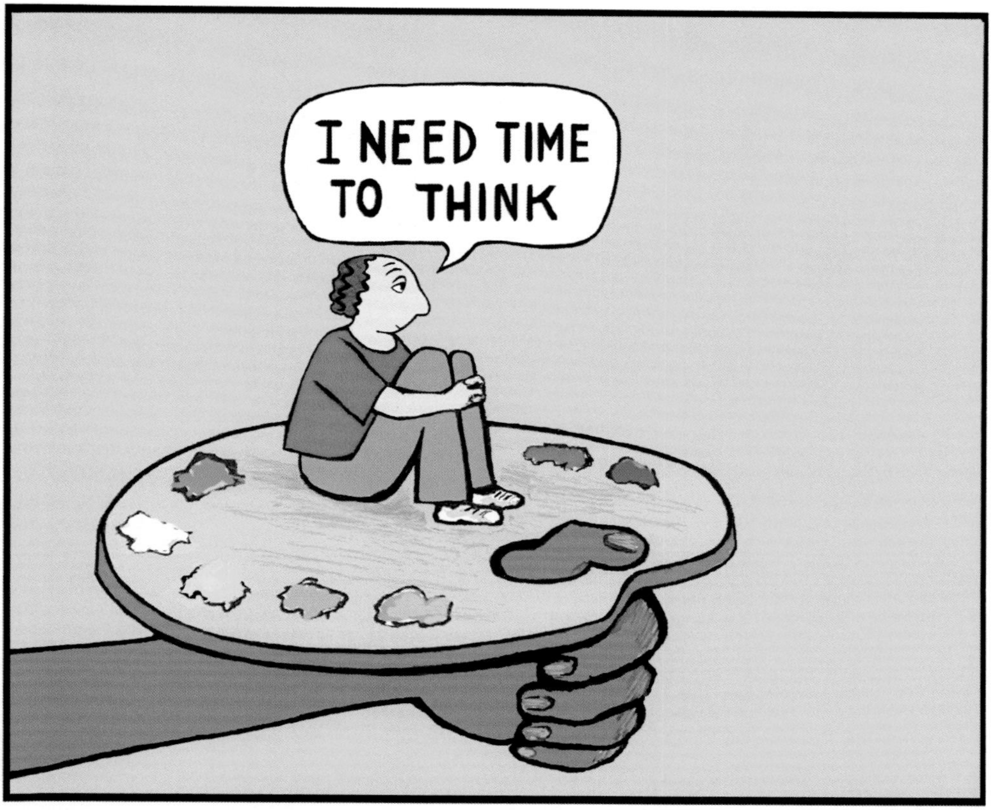
I NEED TIME TO THINK

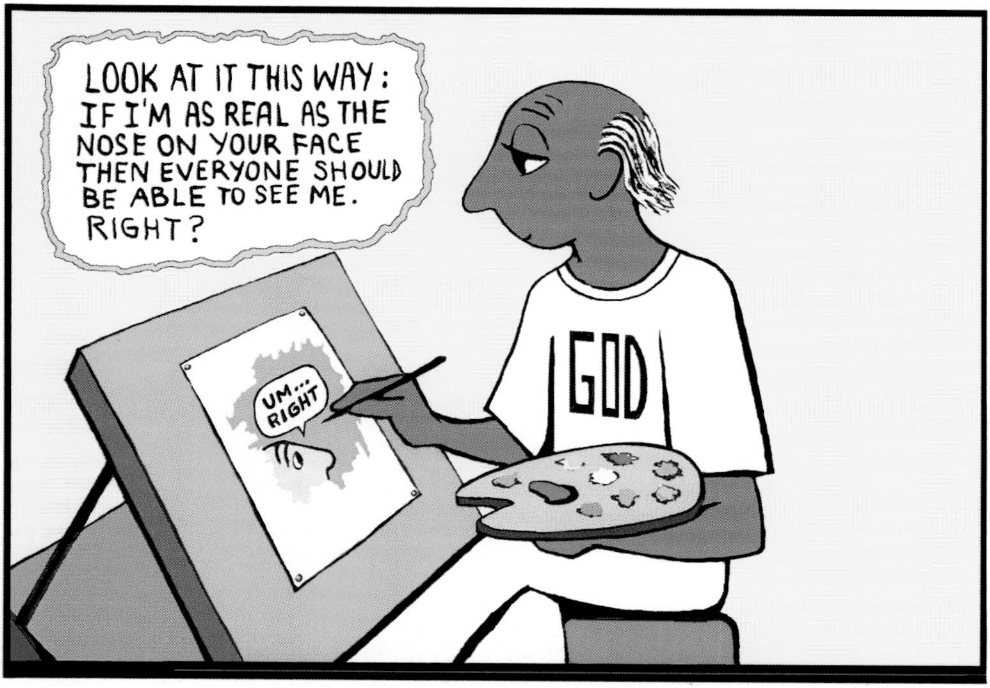
LOOK AT IT THIS WAY: IF I'M AS REAL AS THE NOSE ON YOUR FACE THEN EVERYONE SHOULD BE ABLE TO SEE ME. RIGHT?
UM... RIGHT
GOD

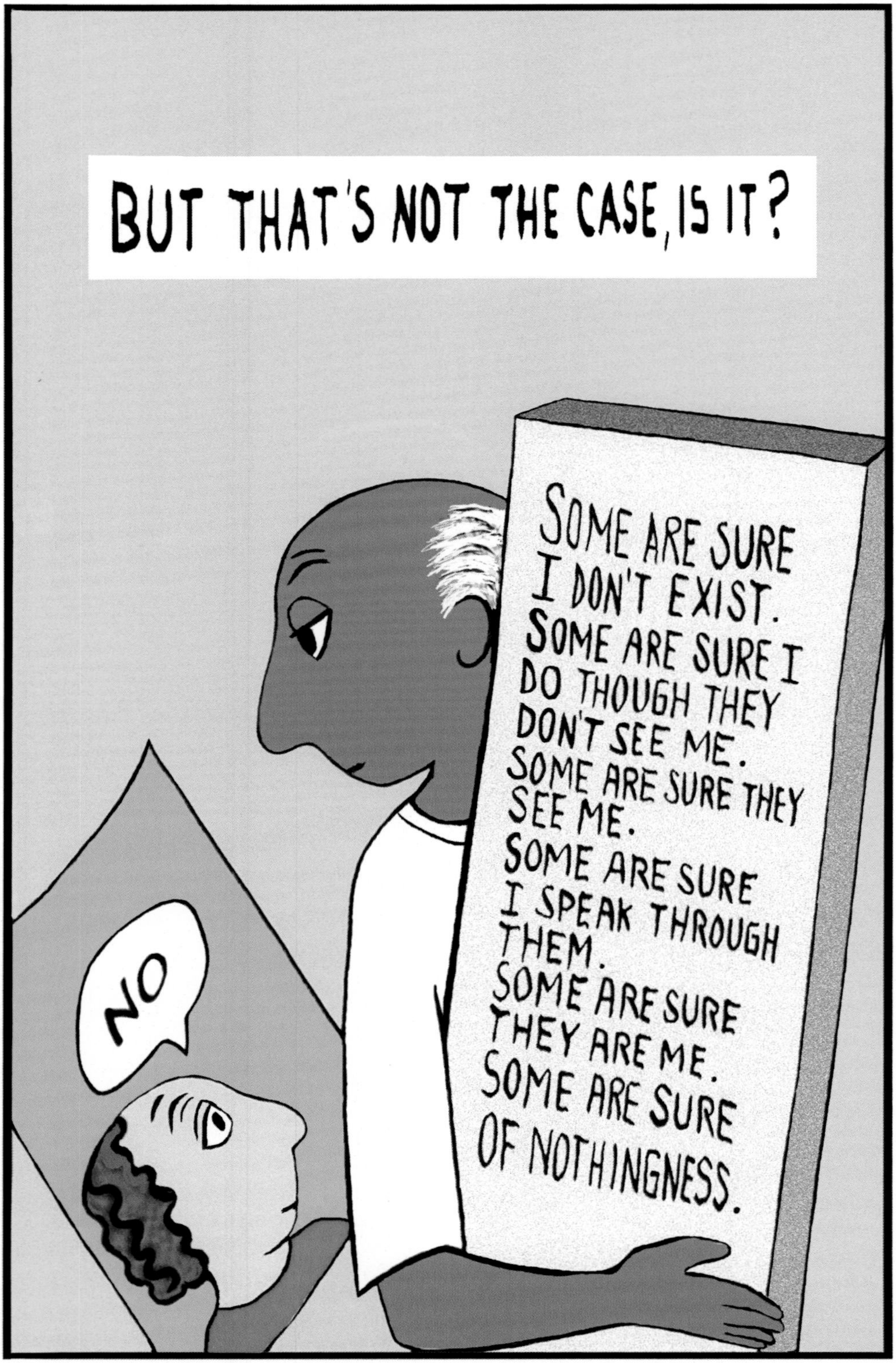
BUT THAT'S NOT THE CASE, IS IT?
SOME ARE SURE I DON'T EXIST. SOME ARE SURE I DO THOUGH THEY DON'T SEE ME. SOME ARE SURE THEY SEE ME. SOME ARE SURE I SPEAK THROUGH THEM. SOME ARE SURE THEY ARE ME. SOME ARE SURE OF NOTHINGNESS.
NO

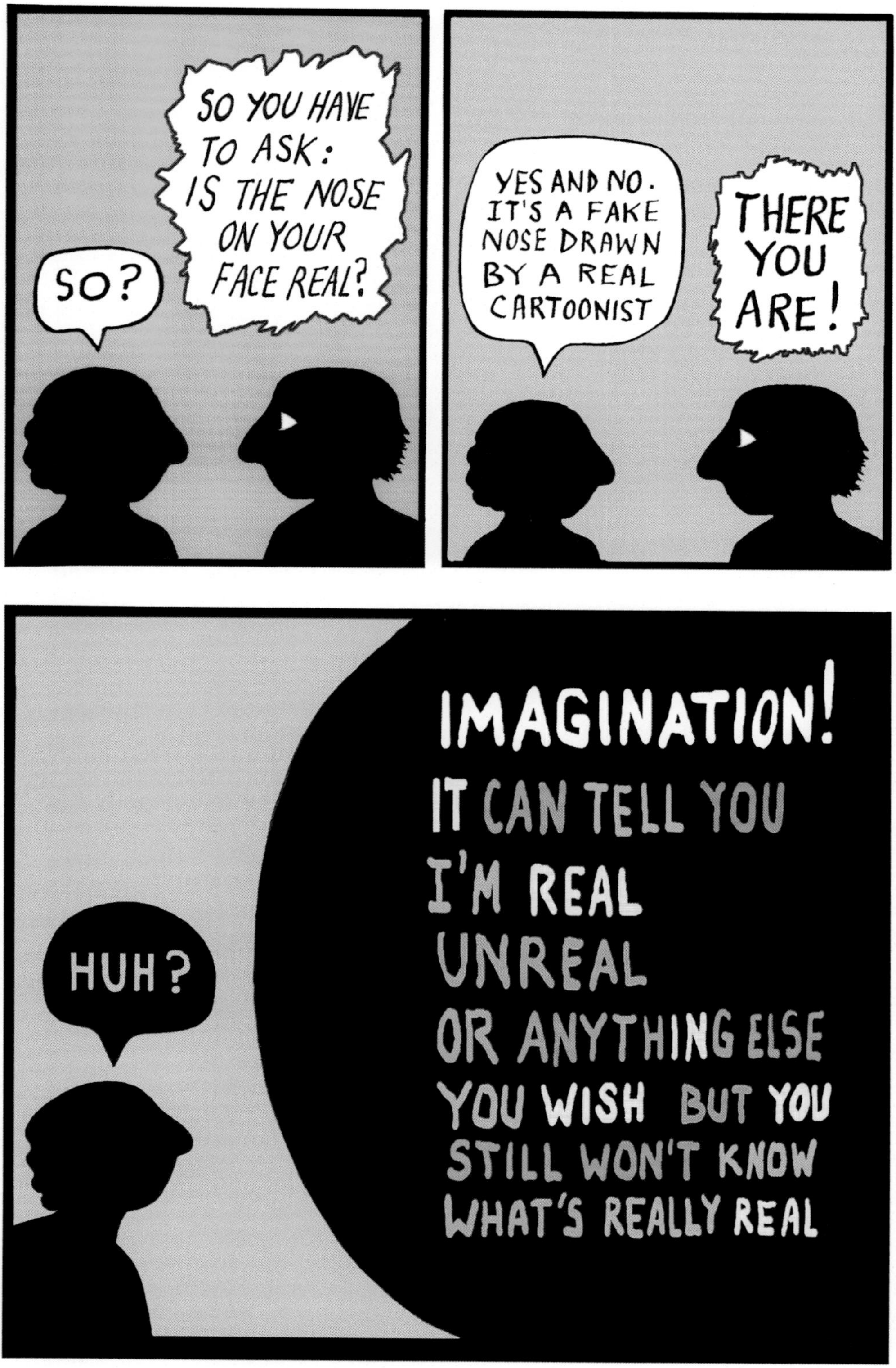
SO?
SO YOU HAVE TO ASK: IS THE NOSE ON YOUR FACE REAL?
YES AND NO. IT'S A FAKE NOSE DRAWN BY A REAL CARTOONIST
THERE YOU ARE!
HUH?
IMAGINATION! IT CAN TELL YOU I'M REAL UNREAL OR ANYTHING ELSE YOU WISH BUT YOU STILL WON'T KNOW WHAT'S REALLY REAL

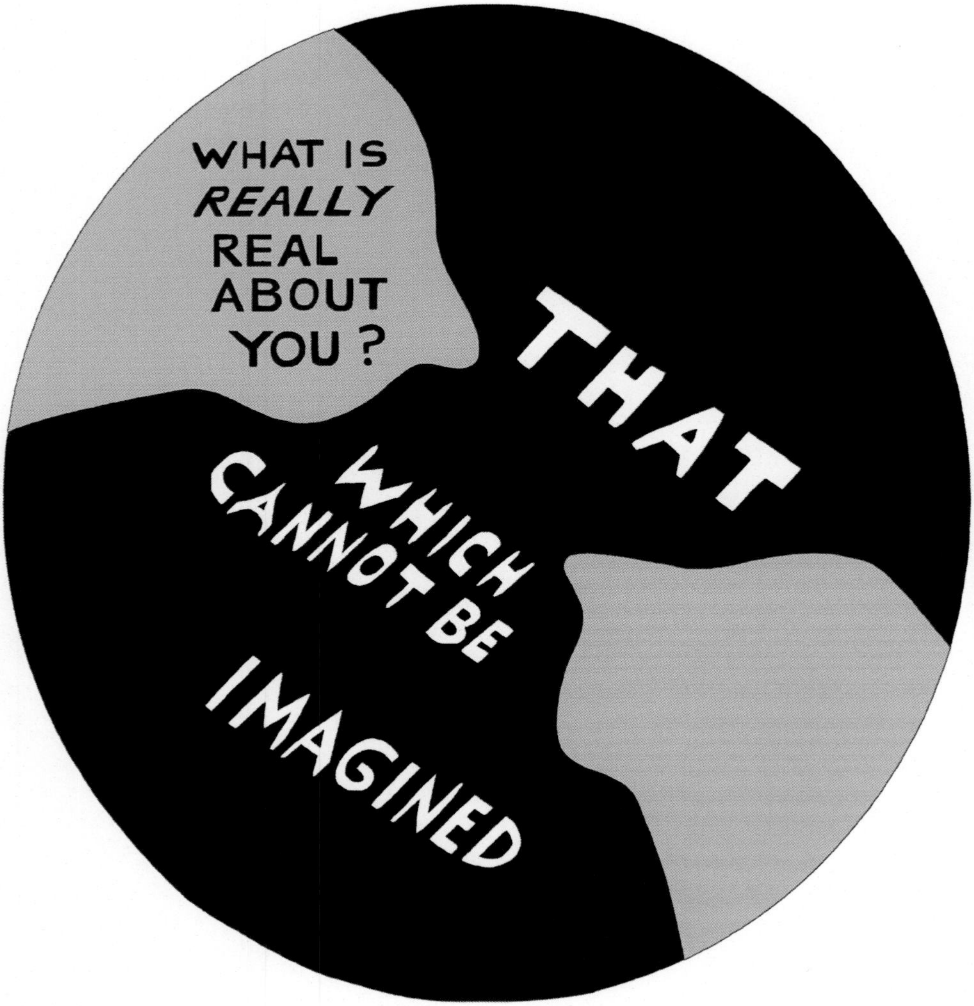
WHAT IS
REALLY
REAL
ABOUT
YOU ?
THAT
WHICH
CANNOT BE
IMAGINED

THIRTEEN

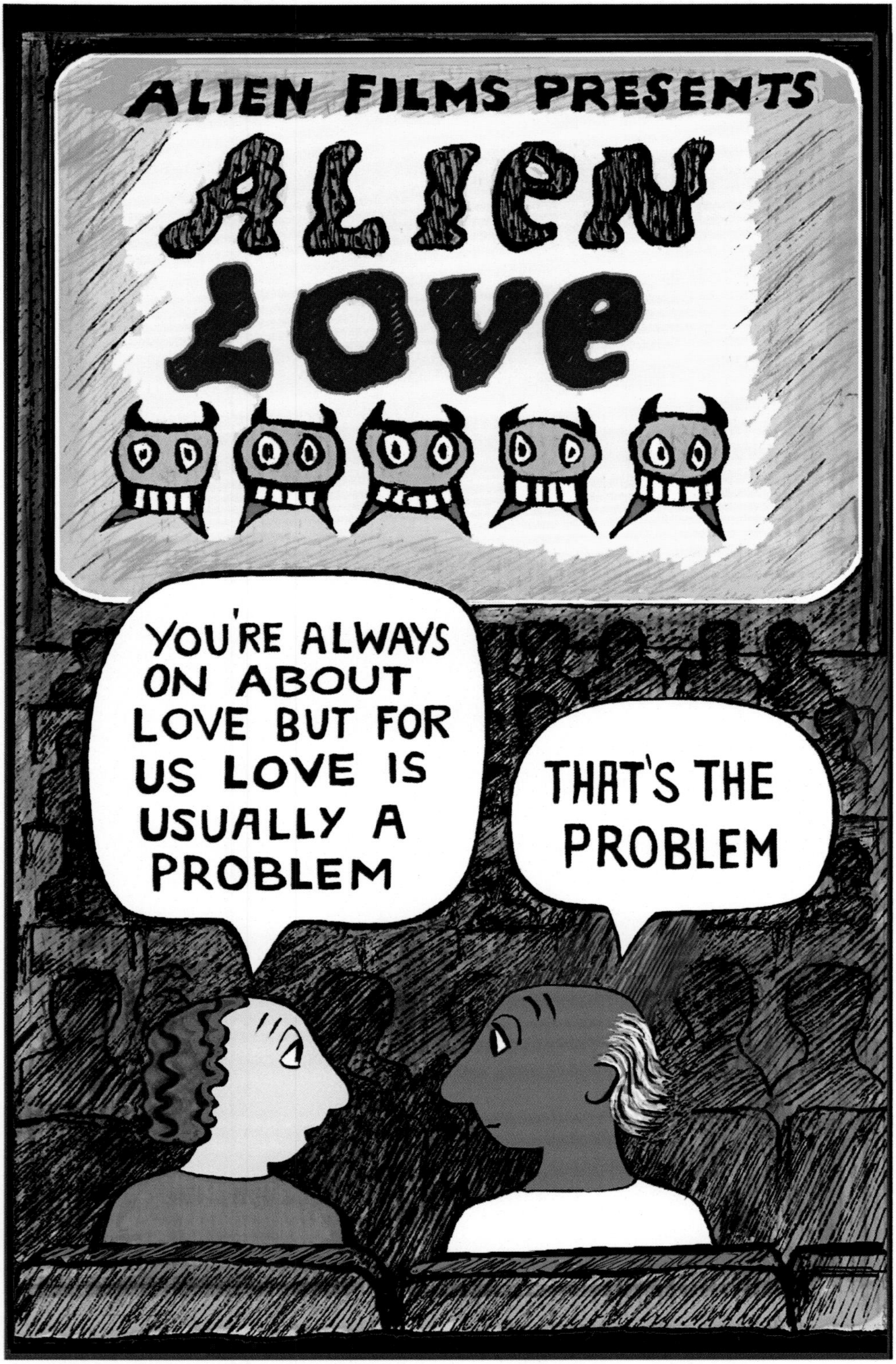
ALIEN FILMS PRESENTS
ALIEN LOVE
YOU'RE ALWAYS ON ABOUT LOVE BUT FOR US LOVE IS USUALLY A PROBLEM
THAT'S THE PROBLEM

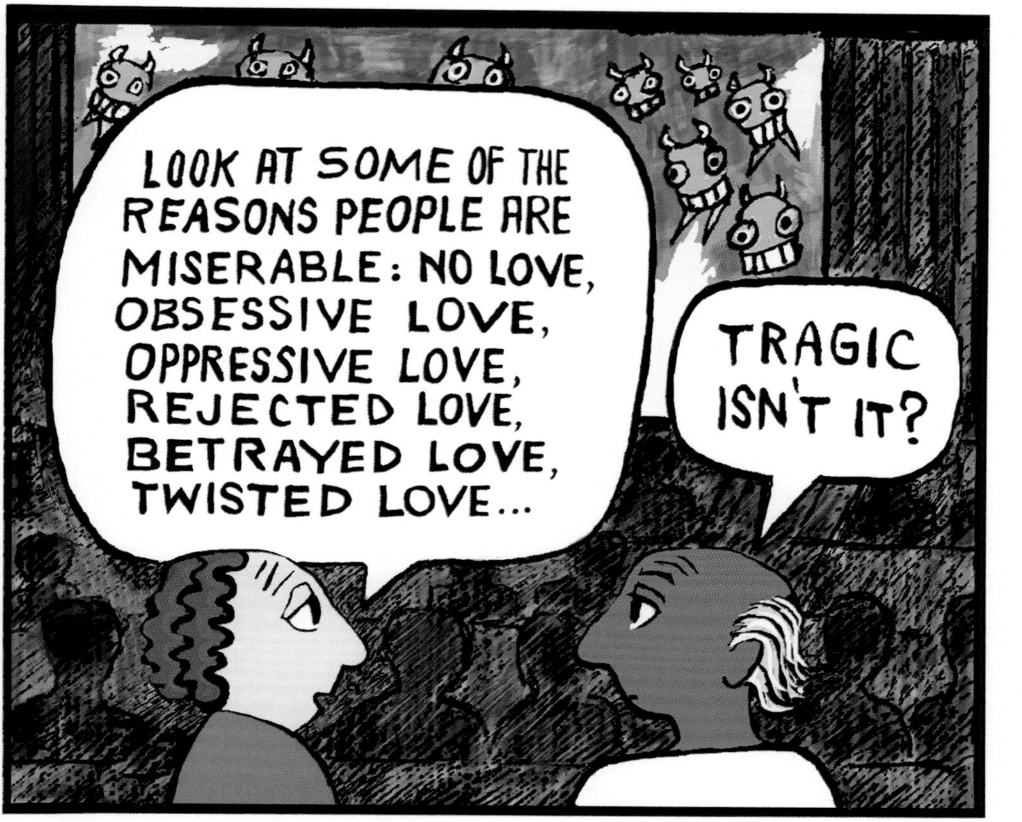
LOOK AT SOME OF THE REASONS PEOPLE ARE MISERABLE: NO LOVE, OBSESSIVE LOVE, OPPRESSIVE LOVE, REJECTED LOVE, BETRAYED LOVE, TWISTED LOVE...
TRAGIC ISN'T IT?

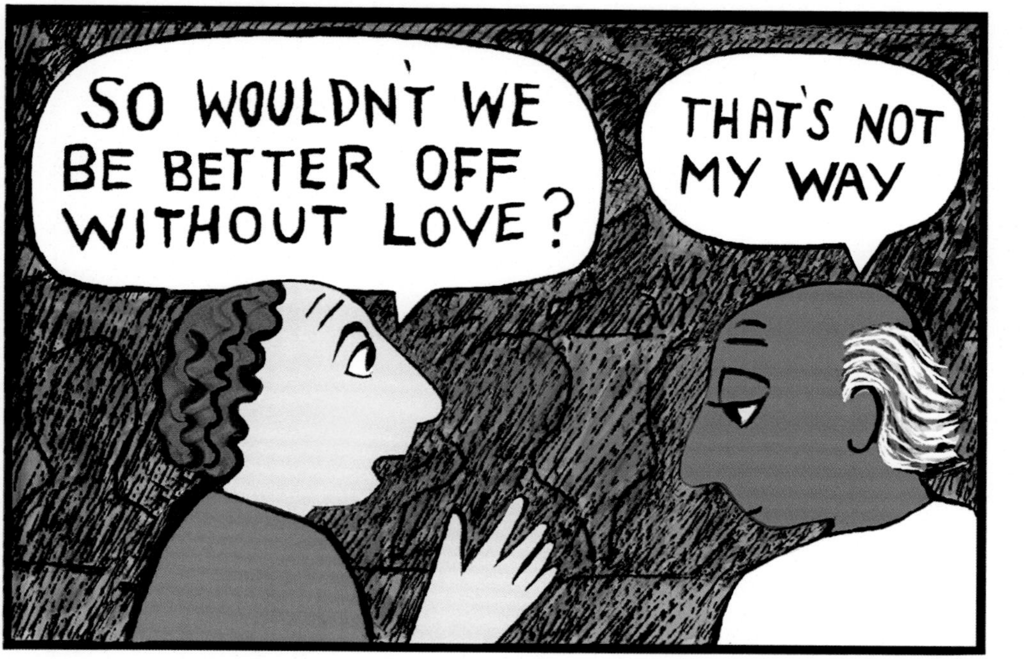
SO WOULDN'T WE BE BETTER OFF WITHOUT LOVE?
THAT'S NOT MY WAY

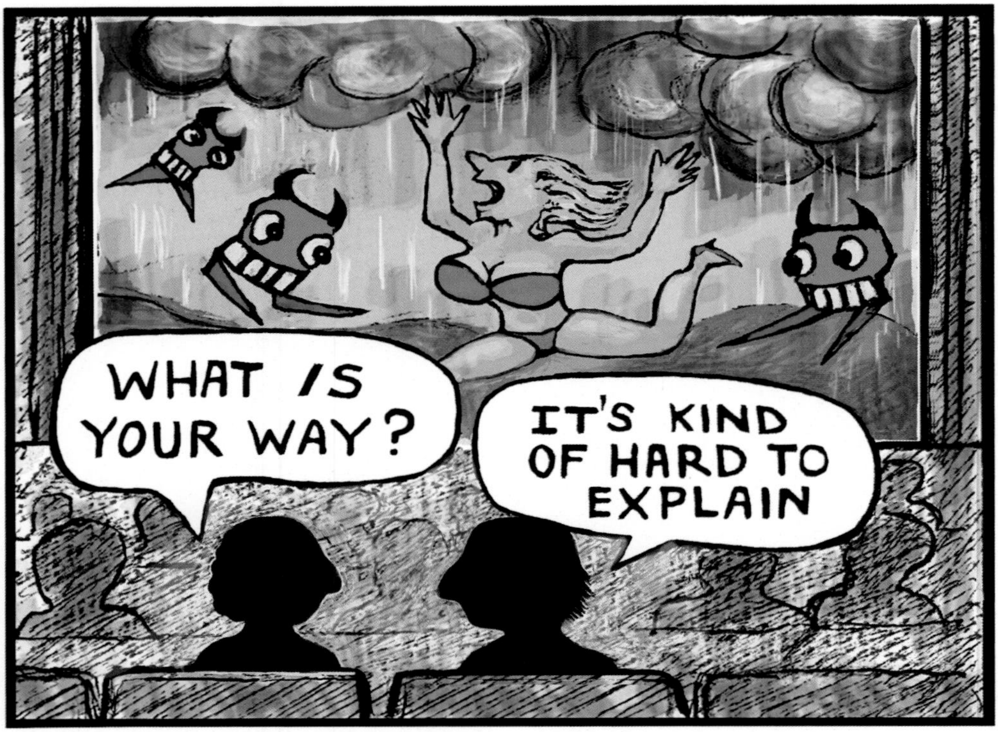
WHAT IS YOUR WAY?
IT'S KIND OF HARD TO EXPLAIN

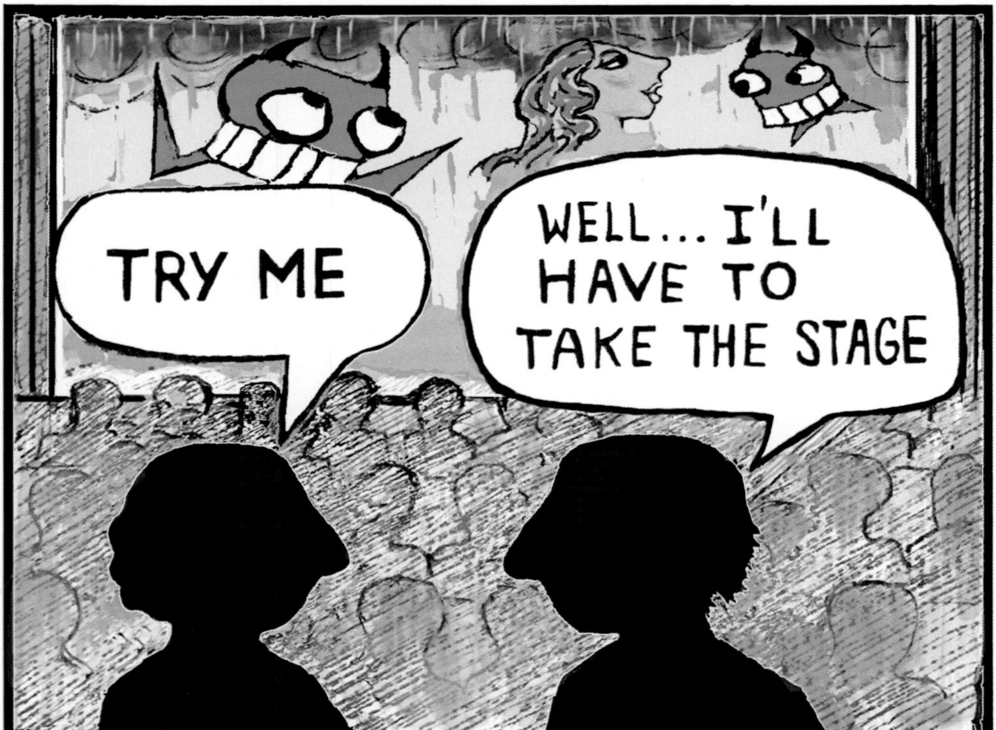
TRY ME
WELL... I'LL HAVE TO TAKE THE STAGE

HAS forthcoming events

Hampstead Authors' Society

www.hasweb.org

Riding the Internet Revolution

The Writer as Publisher

Illustrated talk by Natalie d'Arbeloff

The internet and digital technology has made it possible for creatives to present their work directly to the public. How can authors, artists, poets and cartoonists benefit from the internet revolution and adapt it to their own ideas and working methods? What steps are needed in order to create, design, print, publish and promote your book? How does print-on-demand work? What are the decisions one must make, the promotional strategies, and the internet resources available?

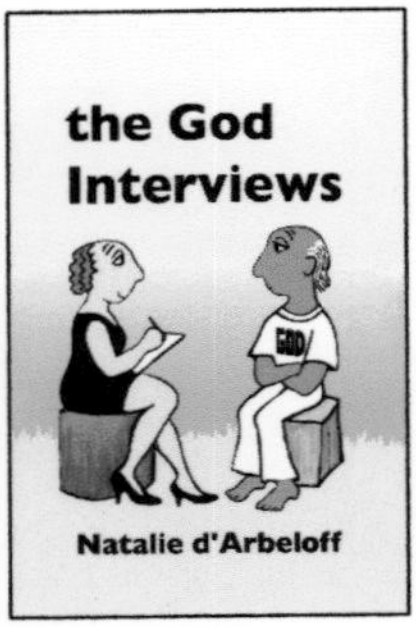

the God Interviews
GOD
Natalie d'Arbeloff

Artist, writer, cartoonist and teacher Natalie d'Arbeloff will discuss all these questions, using as an example her own experience of transforming her online comic strip, *The God Interviews*, into a full-colour book, published by print-on-demand and promoted via her popular blog, *Blaugustine*.

Natalie d'Arbeloff's work is in private and public collections internationally. Her books include: *Creating in Collage, An Artist's Workbook, Designing With Natural Forms, Augustine's True Confession* and *The Joy of Letting Women Down.*

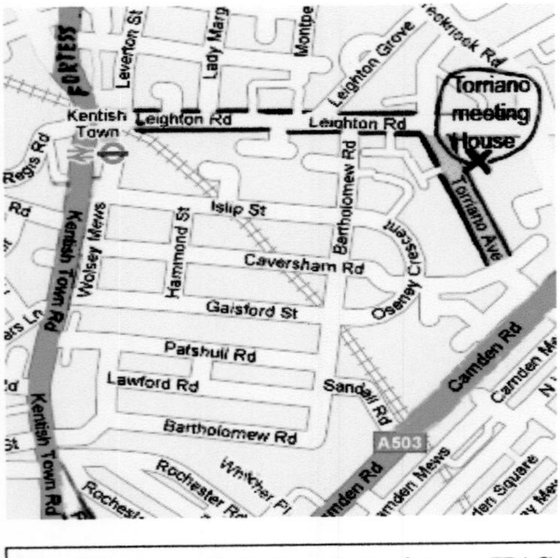

Torriano meeting House
Kentish Town
Leighton Rd
Leighton Rd
Leverton St
Lady Marg
Leighton Grove
Islip St
Bartholomew Rd
Torriano Ave
Kentish Town Rd
Wolsey Mews
Hammond St
Caversham Rd
Gaisford St
Oseney Crescent
Patshull Rd
Lawford Rd
Sandall Rd
Camden Rd
Bartholomew Rd
A503
Rochester Rd
Camden Mews
Camden Square
Kentish Town Rd

PLACE:

The Torriano Meeting House
99 Torriano Avenue, London NW5 2RX

Tube: Kentish Town
Buses: 134, 214, C2, 390, 393

TIME: **14:30 -16:00**

DATE: **Sunday, 24th February**

COST: **£5 at the door**.

The Hampstead Authors' Society – **HAS** for short – was founded 10 years ago. It is a society for authors, artists, journalists, academics, photographers, actors, filmmakers, translators – people from a wide variety of creative backgrounds, from Hampstead and well beyond. More info: ***www.hasweb.org***

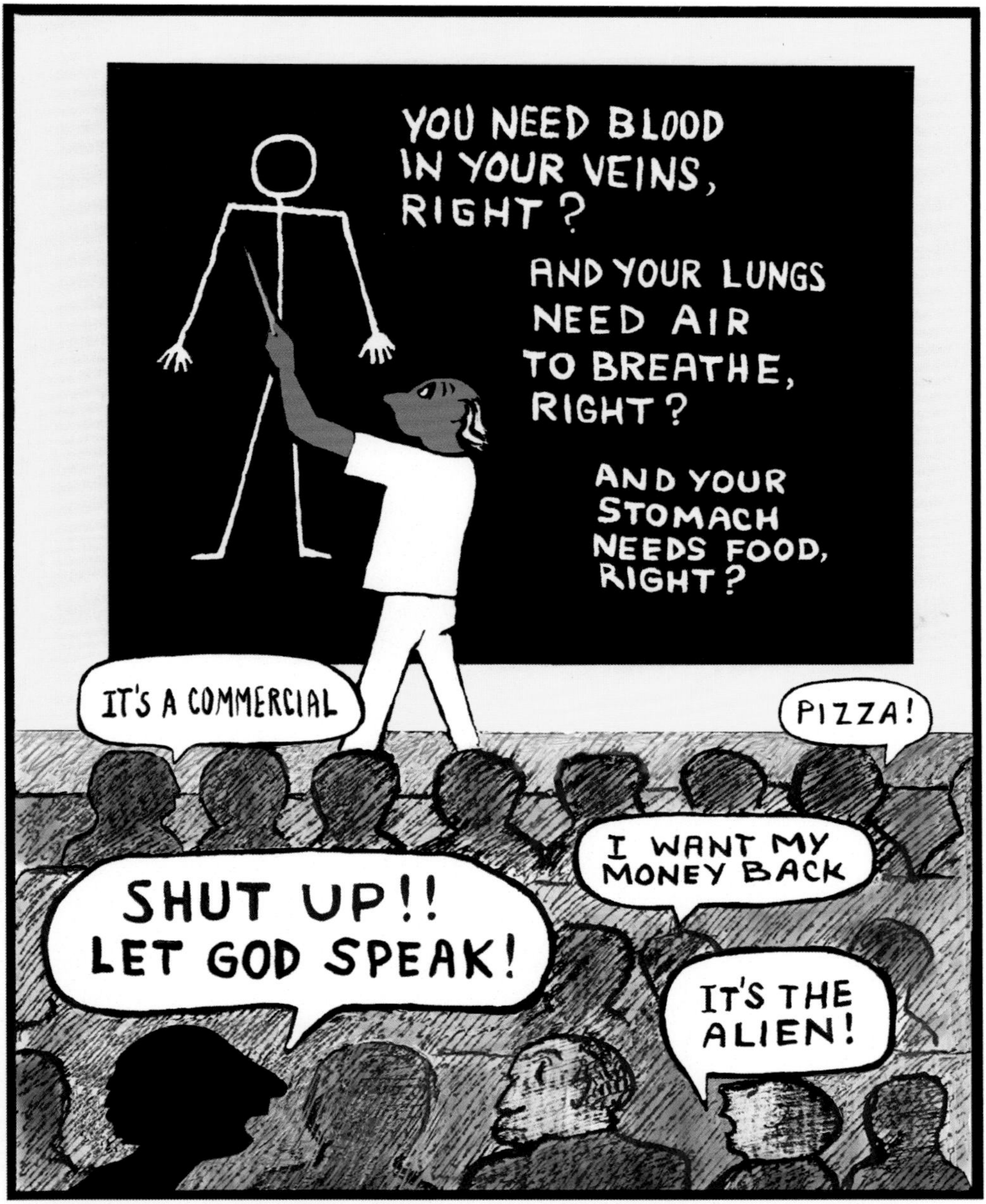
YOU NEED BLOOD IN YOUR VEINS, RIGHT?
AND YOUR LUNGS NEED AIR TO BREATHE, RIGHT?
AND YOUR STOMACH NEEDS FOOD, RIGHT?
IT'S A COMMERCIAL
PIZZA!
I WANT MY MONEY BACK
SHUT UP!! LET GOD SPEAK!
IT'S THE ALIEN!

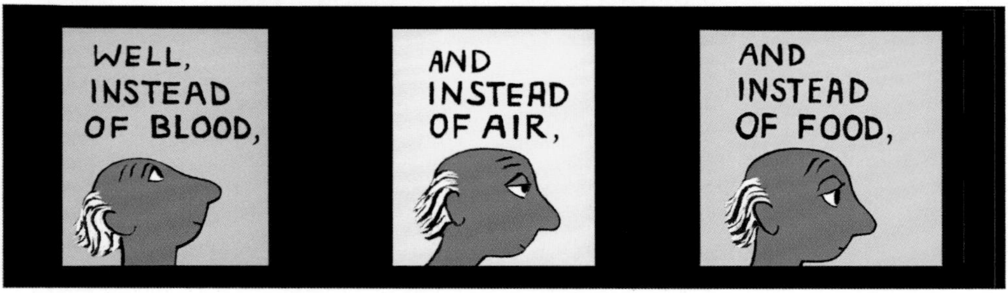
WELL, INSTEAD OF BLOOD,
AND INSTEAD OF AIR,
AND INSTEAD OF FOOD,

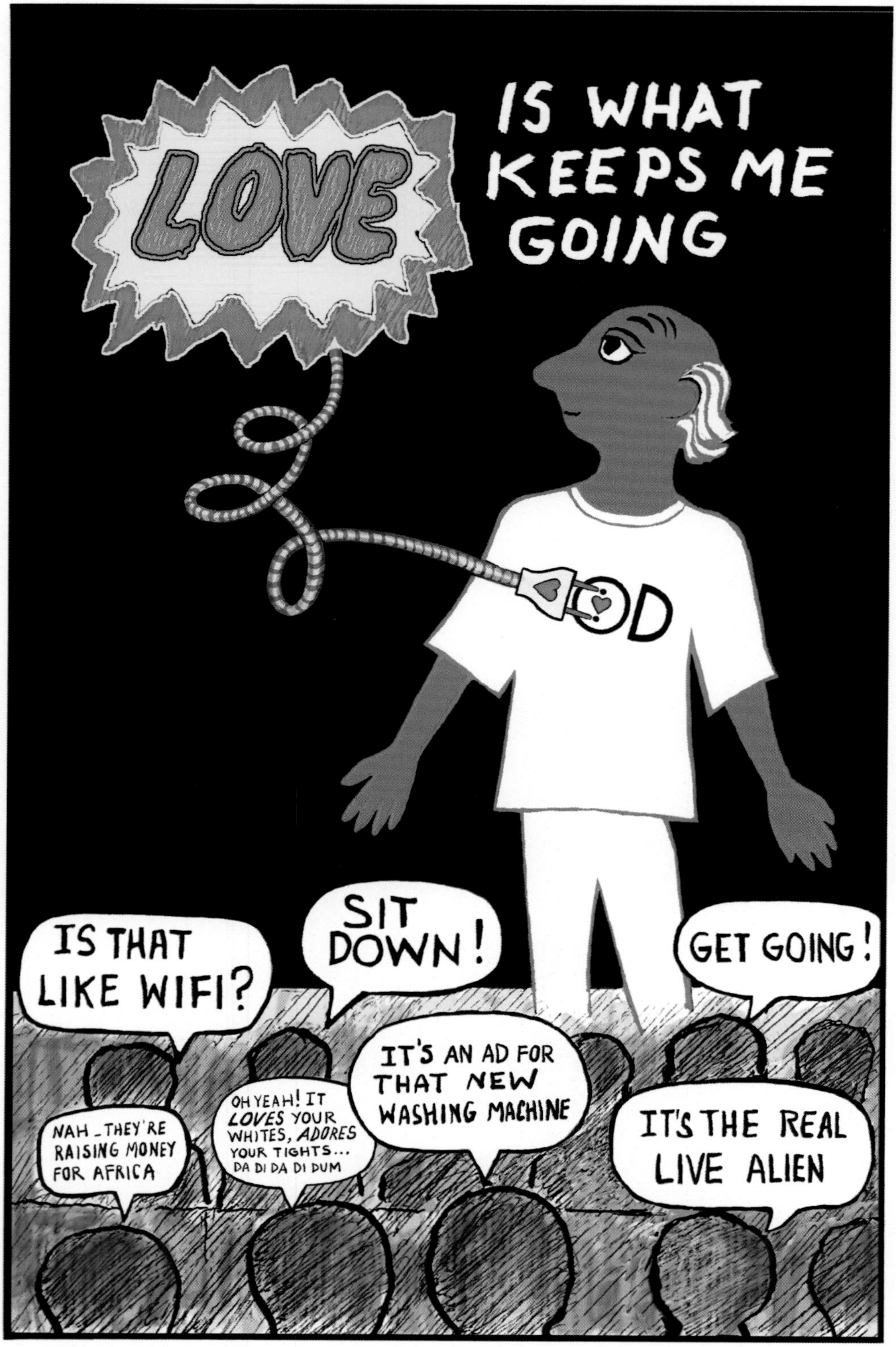
LOVE
IS WHAT KEEPS ME GOING
OD
IS THAT LIKE WIFI?
SIT DOWN!
GET GOING!
NAH - THEY'RE RAISING MONEY FOR AFRICA
OH YEAH! IT *LOVES* YOUR WHITES, *ADORES* YOUR TIGHTS... DA DI DA DI DUM
IT'S AN AD FOR THAT *NEW* WASHING MACHINE
IT'S THE REAL LIVE ALIEN

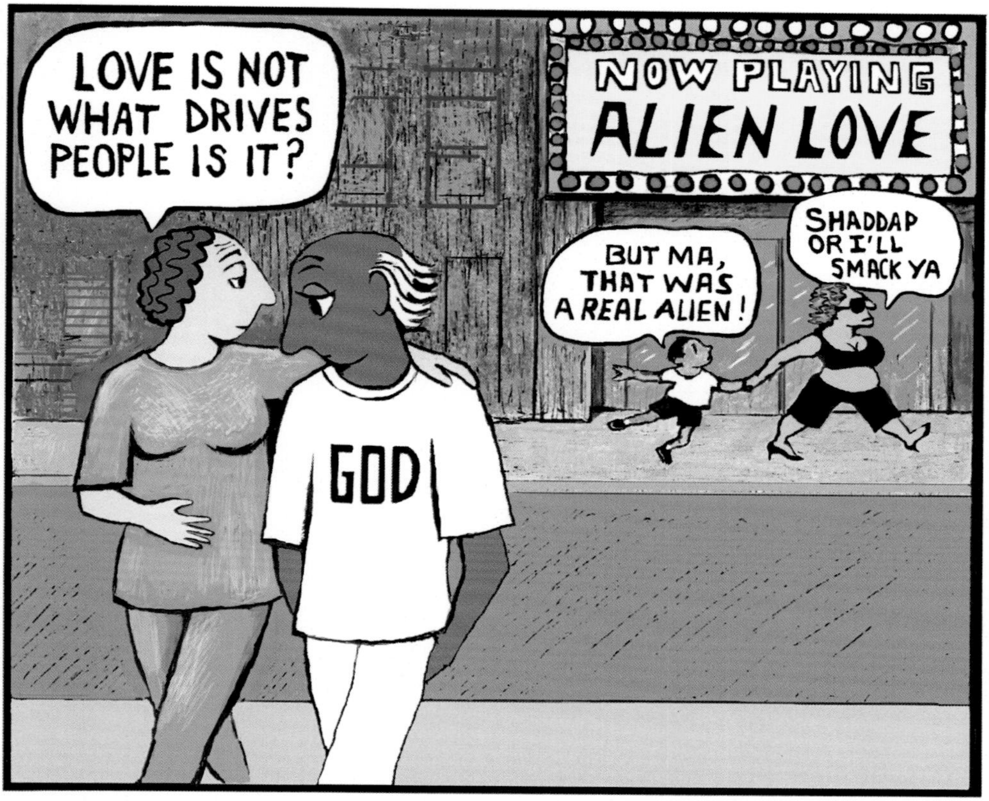
LOVE IS NOT WHAT DRIVES PEOPLE IS IT?
NOW PLAYING ALIEN LOVE
BUT MA, THAT WAS A REAL ALIEN!
SHADDAP OR I'LL SMACK YA
GOD

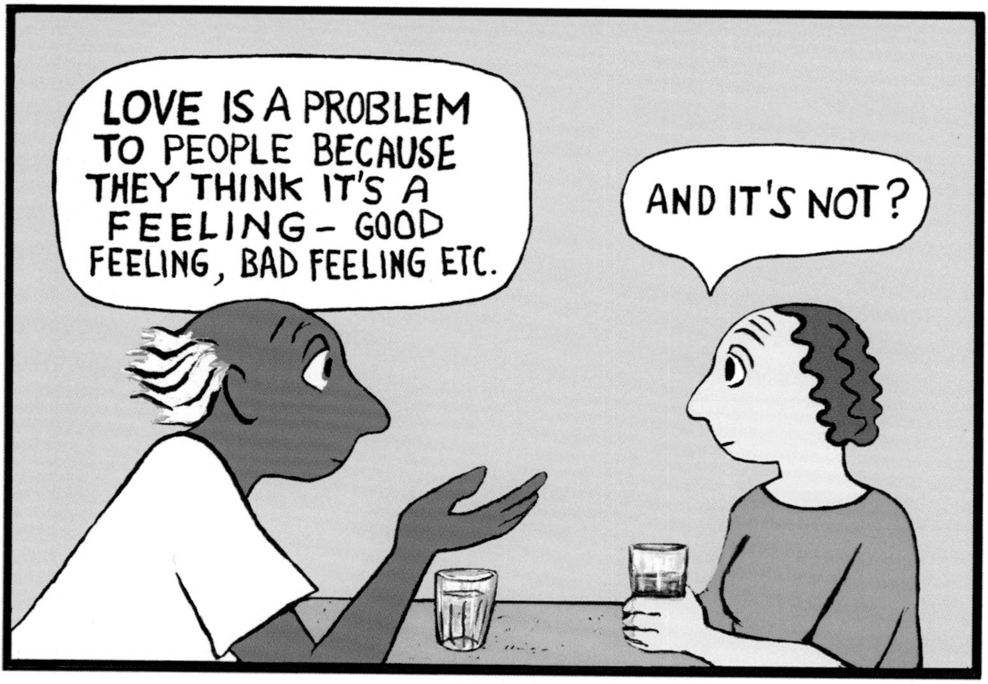
LOVE IS A PROBLEM TO PEOPLE BECAUSE THEY THINK IT'S A FEELING- GOOD FEELING, BAD FEELING ETC.
AND IT'S NOT?

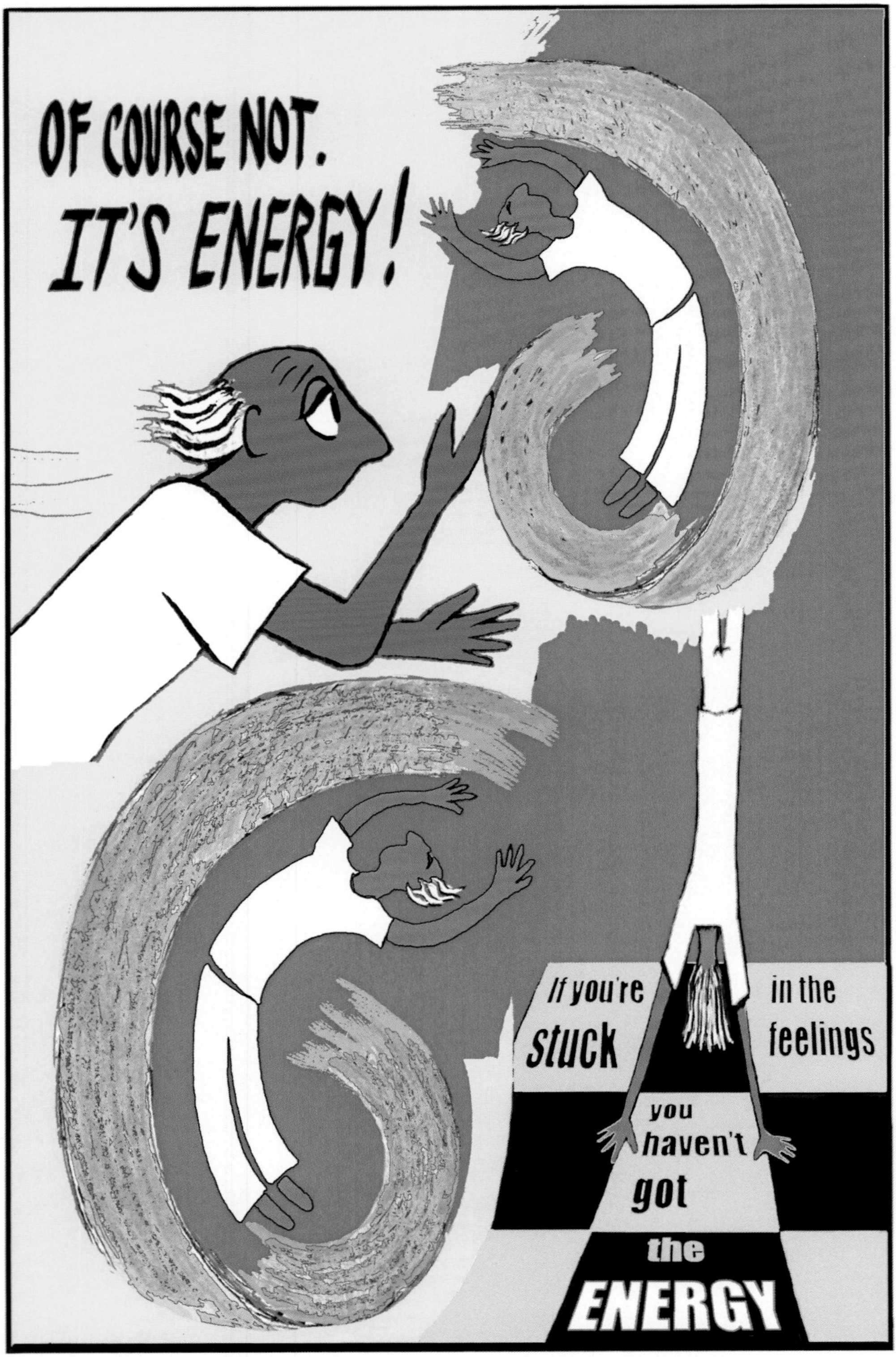
OF COURSE NOT.
IT'S ENERGY!
If you're stuck in the feelings you haven't got the ENERGY

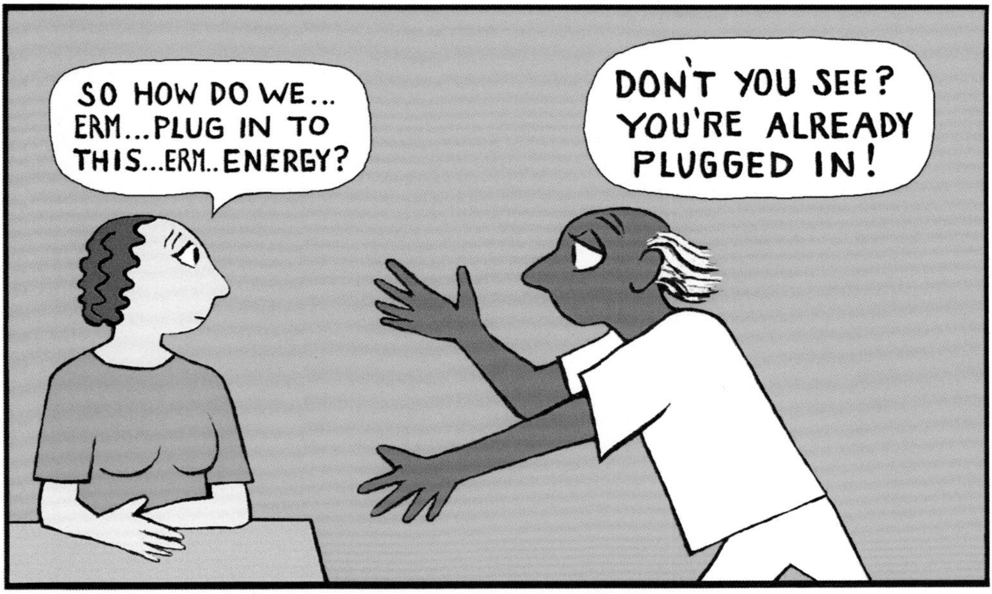
SO HOW DO WE... ERM...PLUG IN TO THIS...ERM..ENERGY?
DON'T YOU SEE? YOU'RE ALREADY PLUGGED IN!

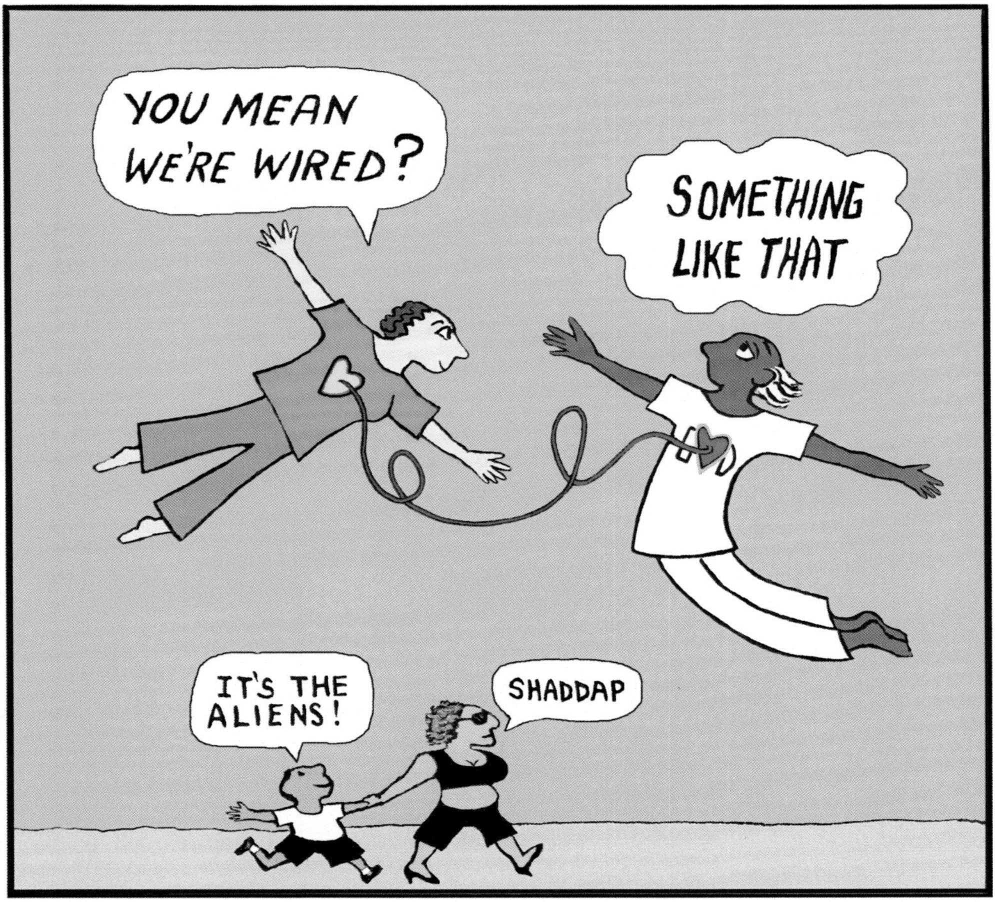
YOU MEAN WE'RE WIRED?
SOMETHING LIKE THAT
IT'S THE ALIENS!
SHADDAP

FOURTEEN

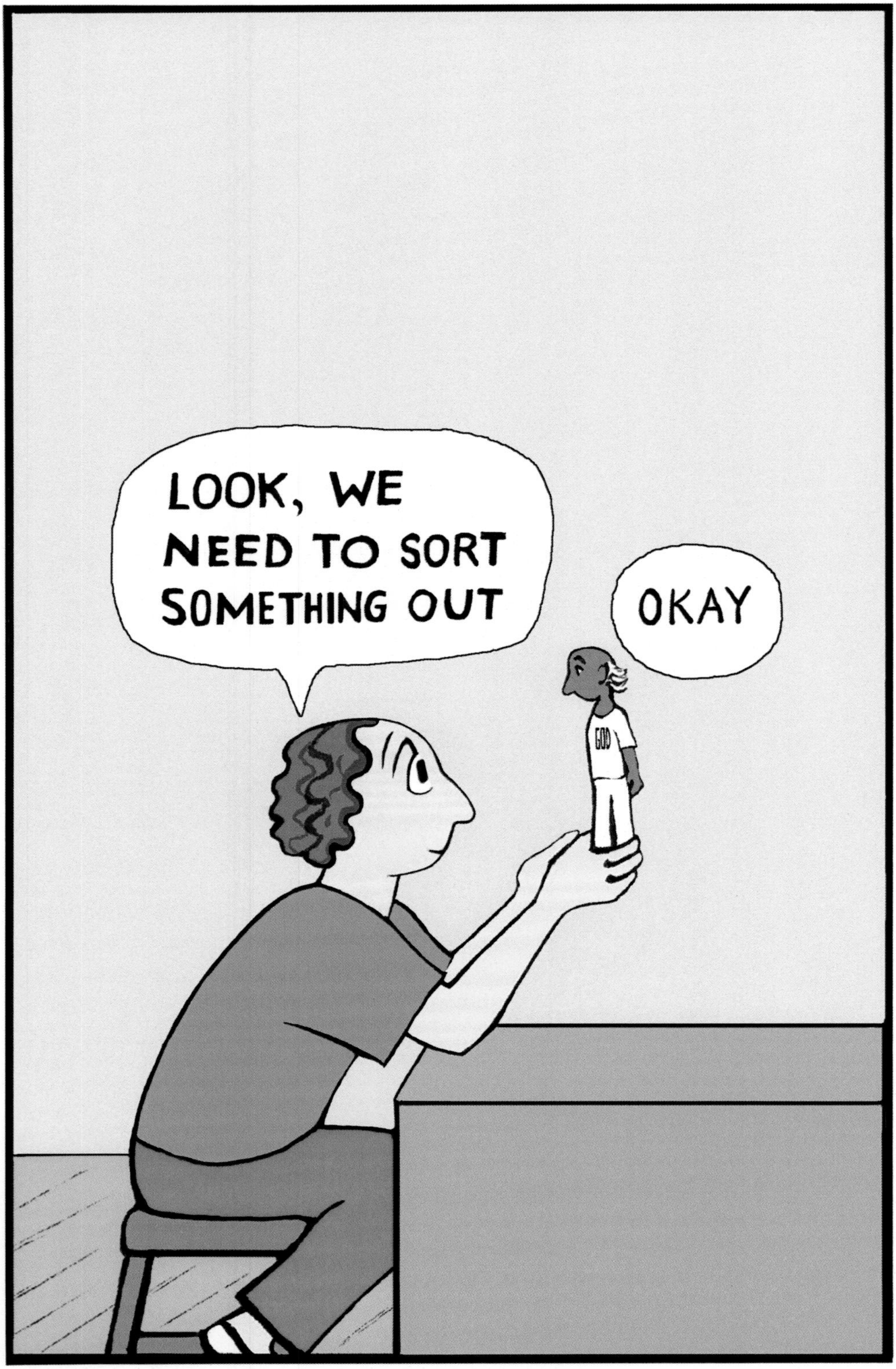
LOOK, WE NEED TO SORT SOMETHING OUT
OKAY
GOD

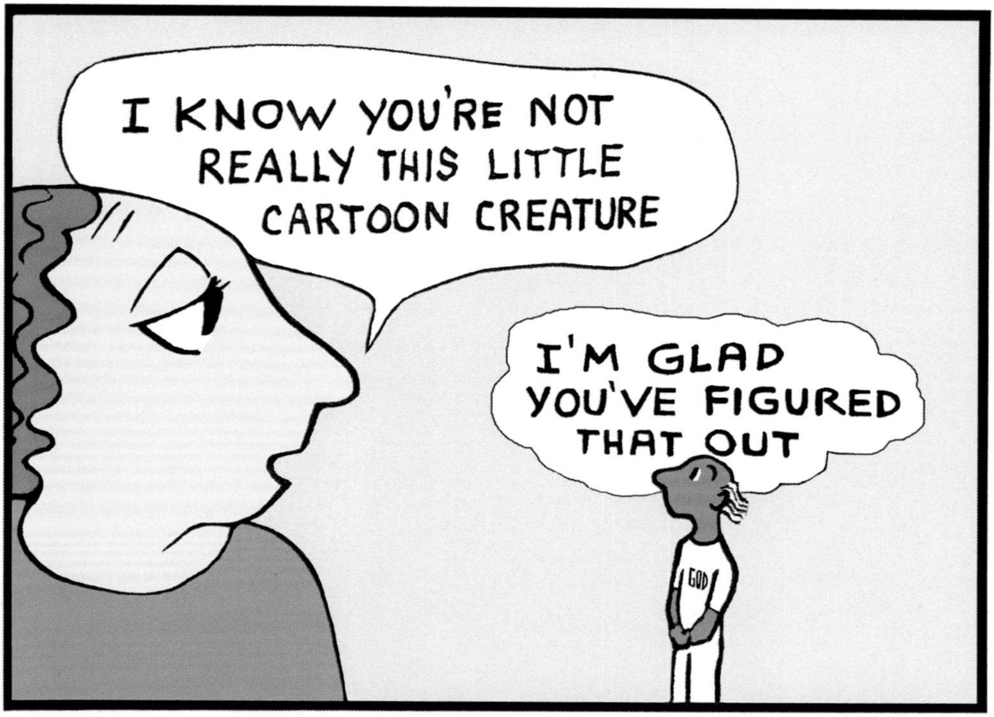
I KNOW YOU'RE NOT REALLY THIS LITTLE CARTOON CREATURE
I'M GLAD YOU'VE FIGURED THAT OUT
GOD

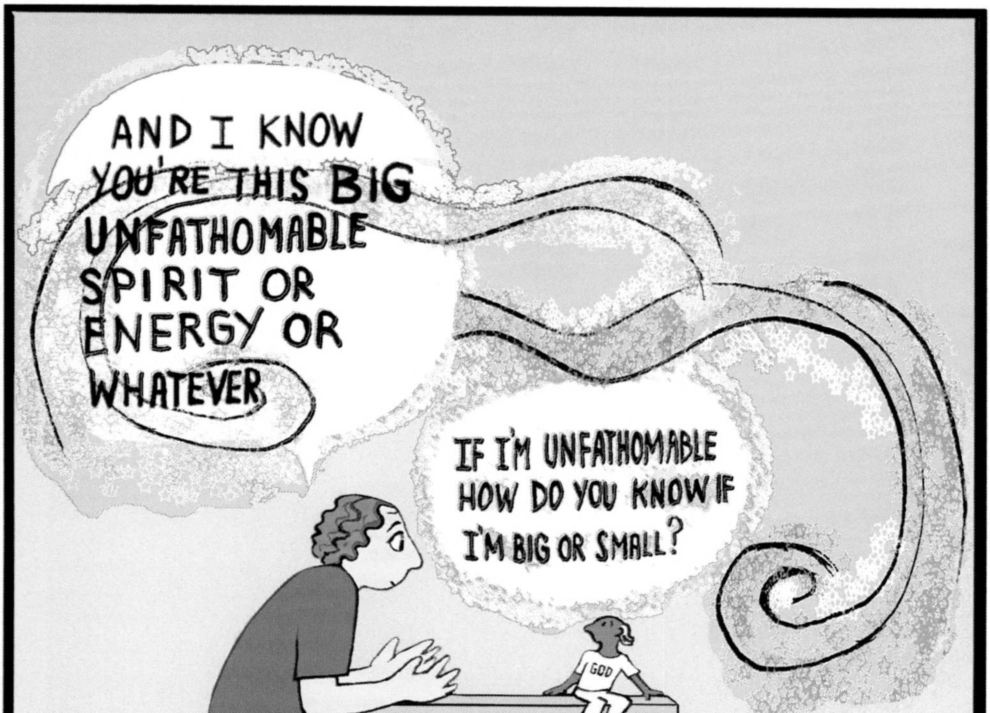
AND I KNOW YOU'RE THIS BIG UNFATHOMABLE SPIRIT OR ENERGY OR WHATEVER
IF I'M UNFATHOMABLE HOW DO YOU KNOW IF I'M BIG OR SMALL?
GOD

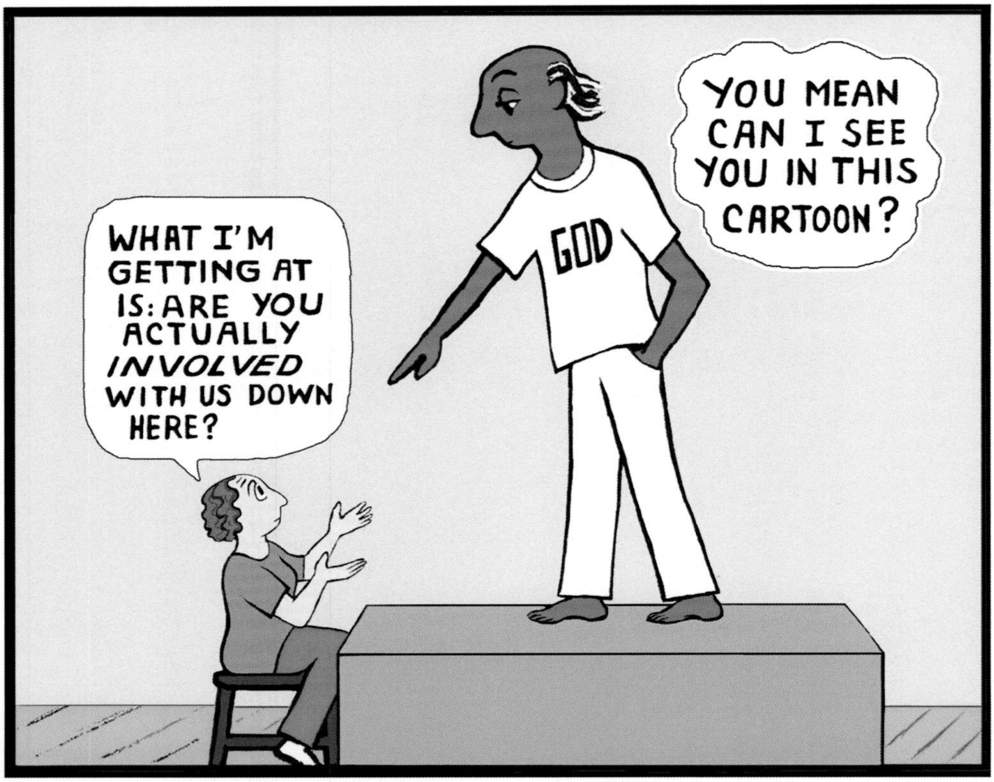
WHAT I'M GETTING AT IS: ARE YOU ACTUALLY *INVOLVED* WITH US DOWN HERE?
YOU MEAN CAN I SEE YOU IN THIS CARTOON?
GOD

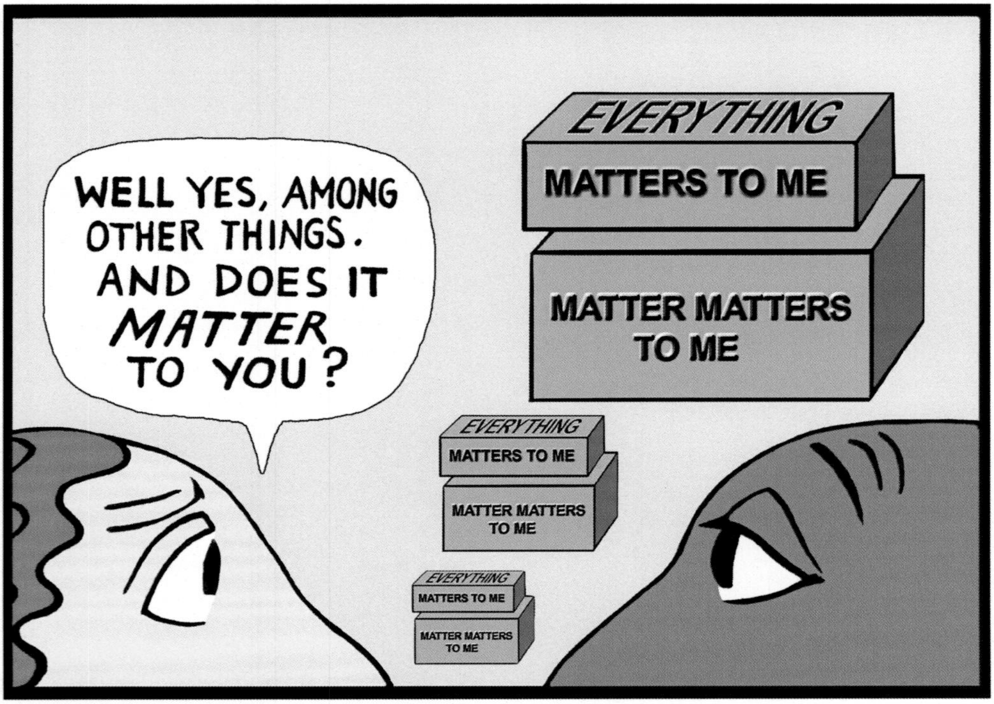
WELL YES, AMONG OTHER THINGS. AND DOES IT *MATTER* TO YOU?
EVERYTHING
MATTERS TO ME
MATTER MATTERS TO ME
EVERYTHING
MATTERS TO ME
MATTER MATTERS TO ME
EVERYTHING
MATTERS TO ME
MATTER MATTERS TO ME

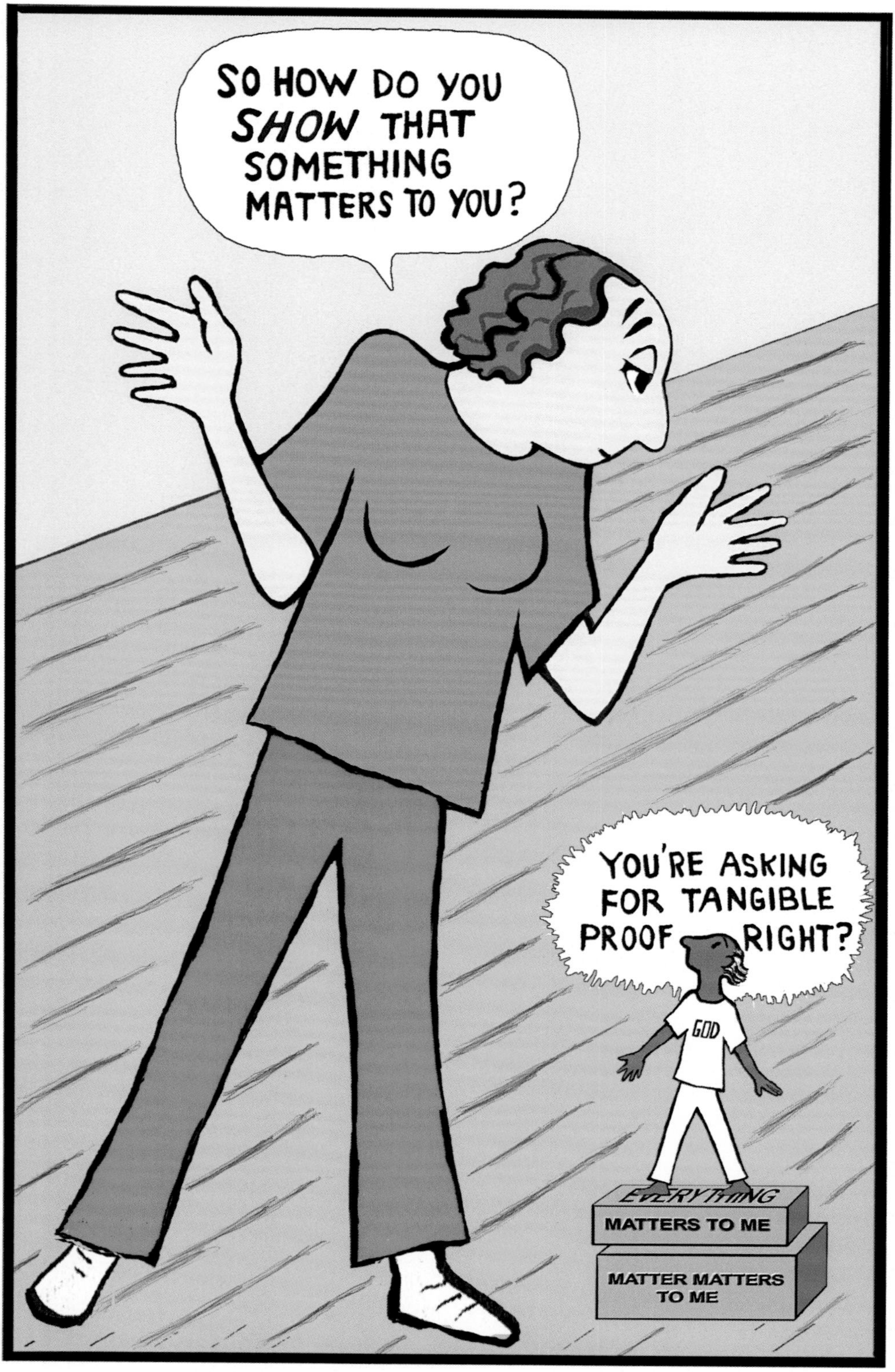
SO HOW DO YOU *SHOW* THAT SOMETHING MATTERS TO YOU?
YOU'RE ASKING FOR TANGIBLE PROOF RIGHT?
GOD
EVERYTHING
MATTERS TO ME
MATTER MATTERS TO ME

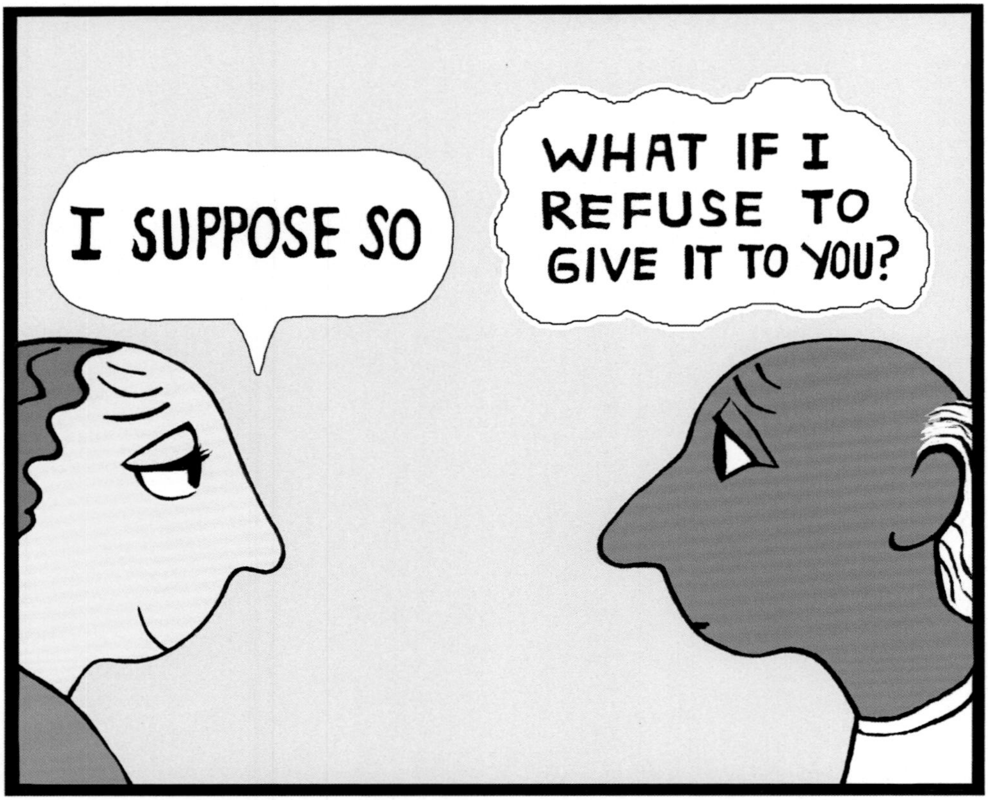
I SUPPOSE SO
WHAT IF I REFUSE TO GIVE IT TO YOU?

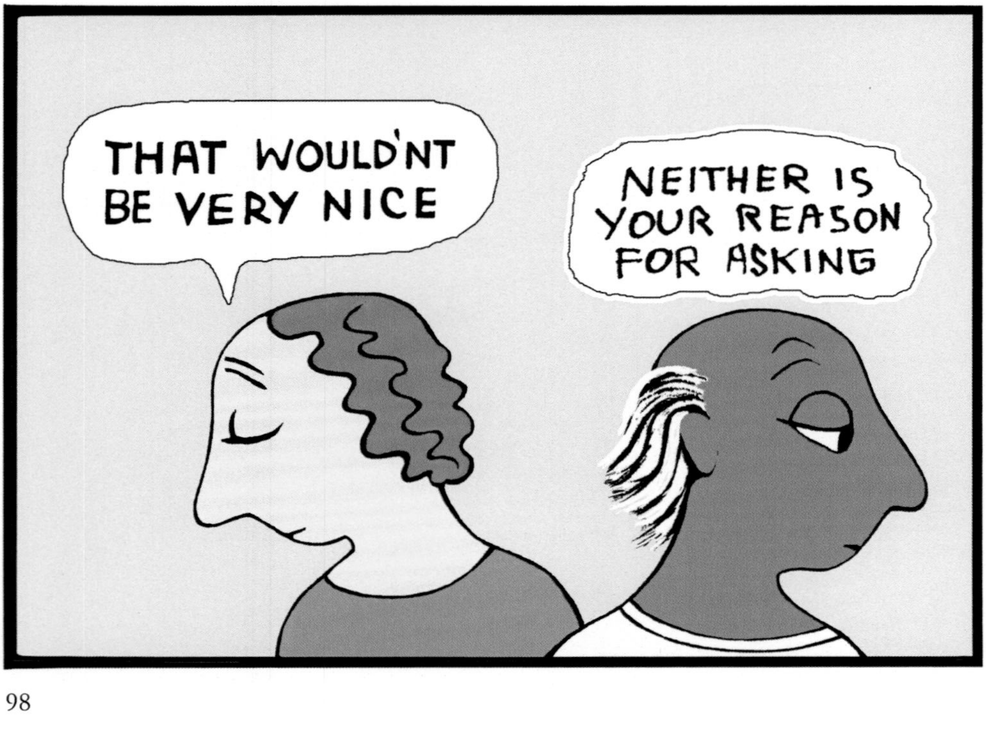
THAT WOULD'NT BE VERY NICE
NEITHER IS YOUR REASON FOR ASKING

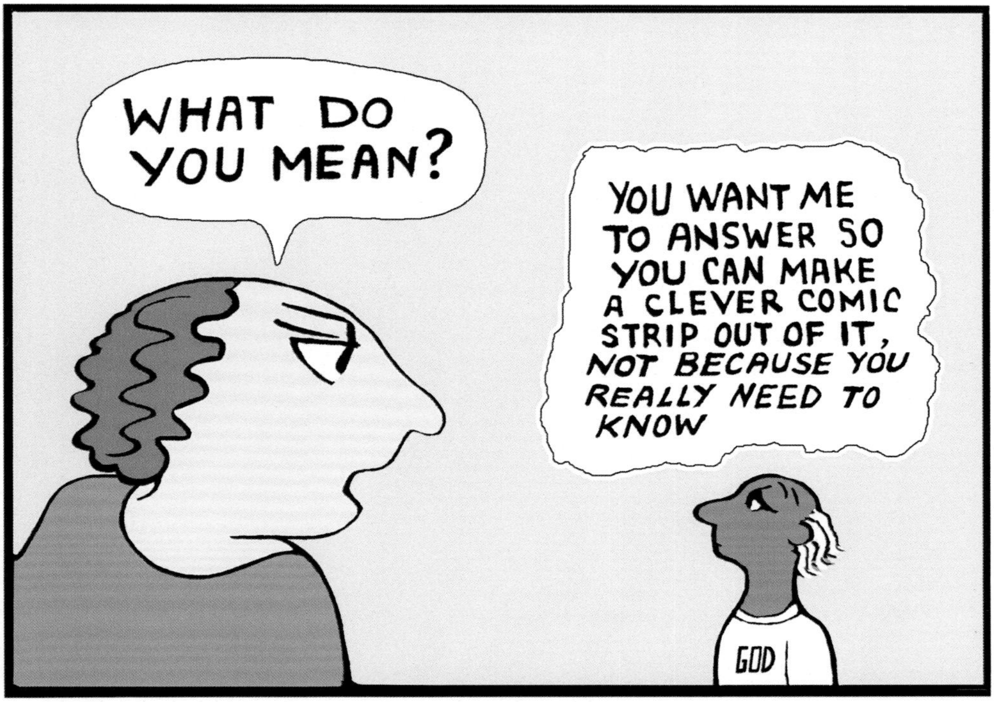
WHAT DO YOU MEAN?
YOU WANT ME TO ANSWER SO YOU CAN MAKE A CLEVER COMIC STRIP OUT OF IT, NOT BECAUSE YOU REALLY NEED TO KNOW
GOD

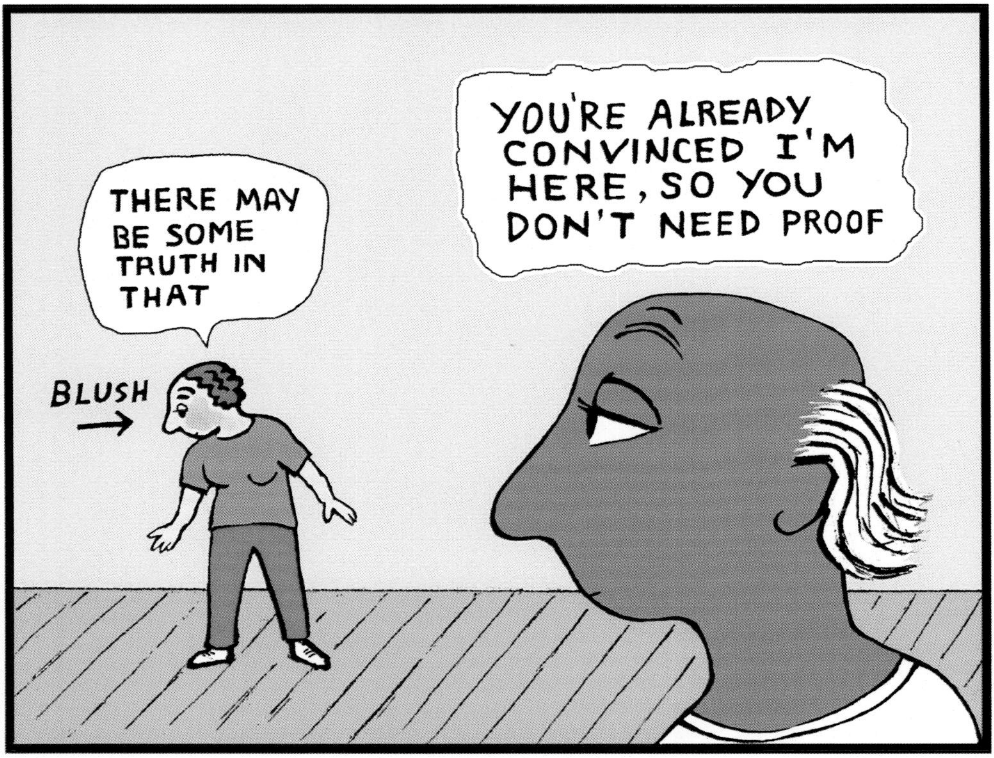
YOU'RE ALREADY CONVINCED I'M HERE, SO YOU DON'T NEED PROOF
THERE MAY BE SOME TRUTH IN THAT
BLUSH

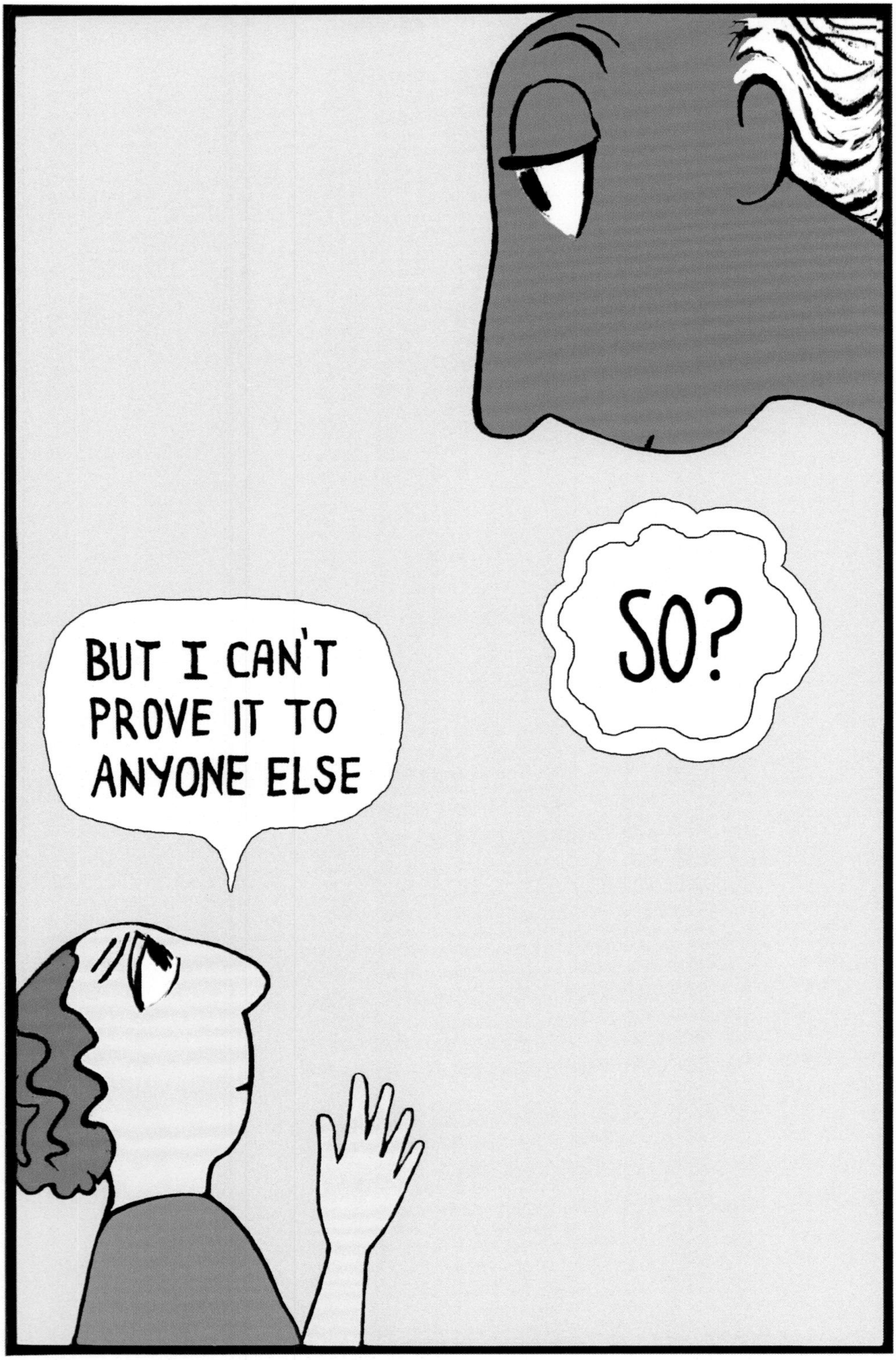
BUT I CAN'T PROVE IT TO ANYONE ELSE
SO?

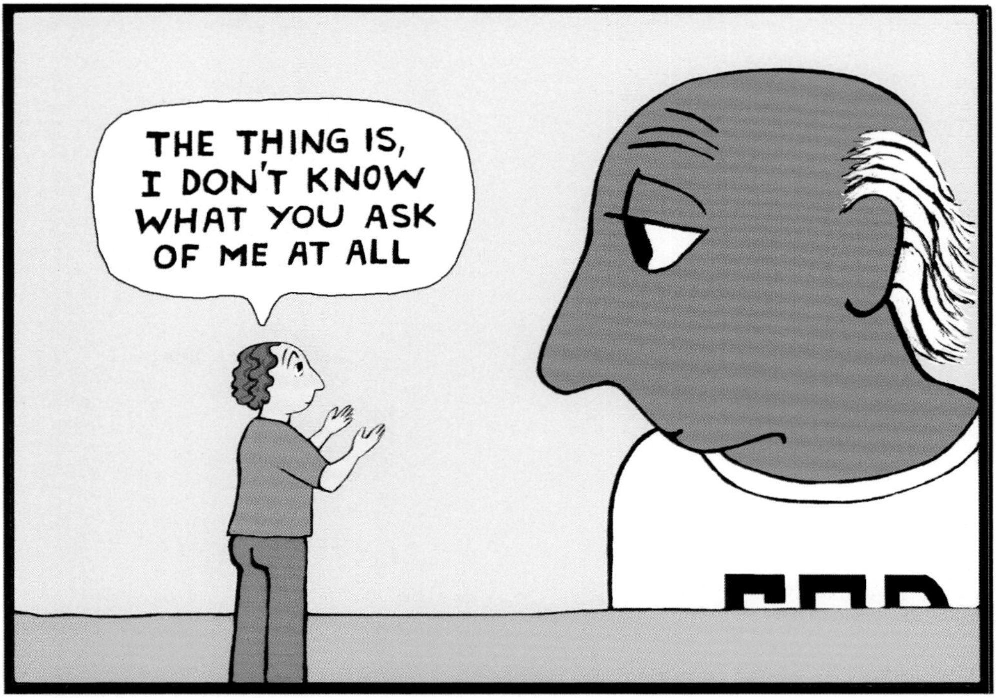
THE THING IS, I DON'T KNOW WHAT YOU ASK OF ME AT ALL

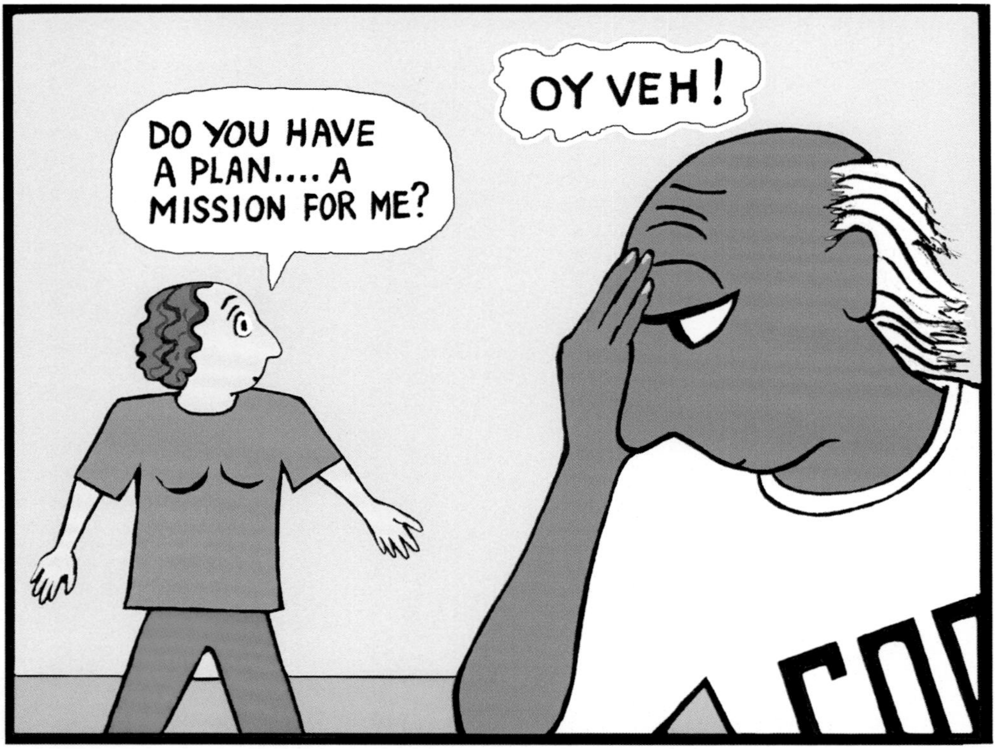
DO YOU HAVE A PLAN.... A MISSION FOR ME?
OY VEH!

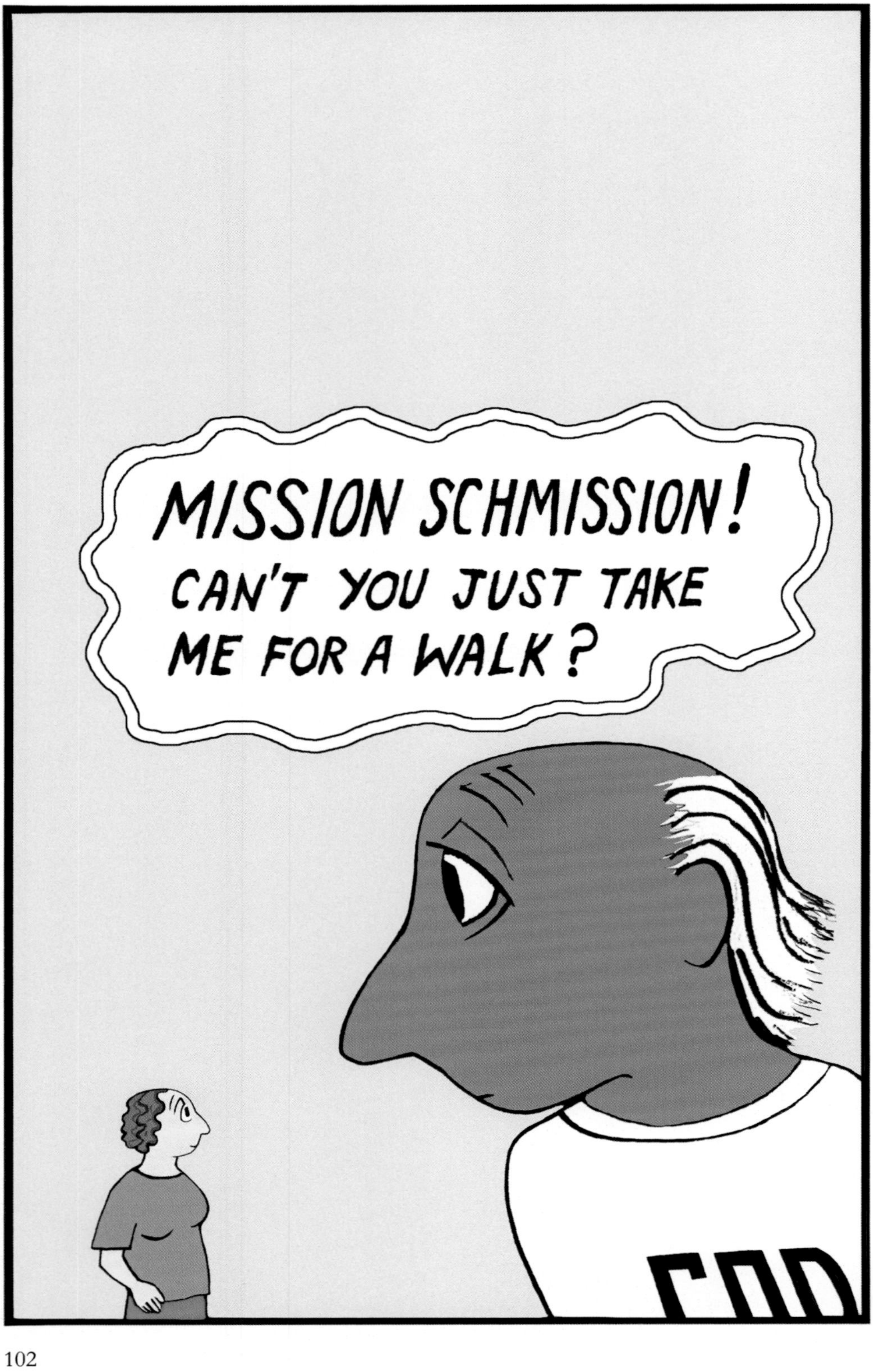
MISSION SCHMISSION!
CAN'T YOU JUST TAKE
ME FOR A WALK?

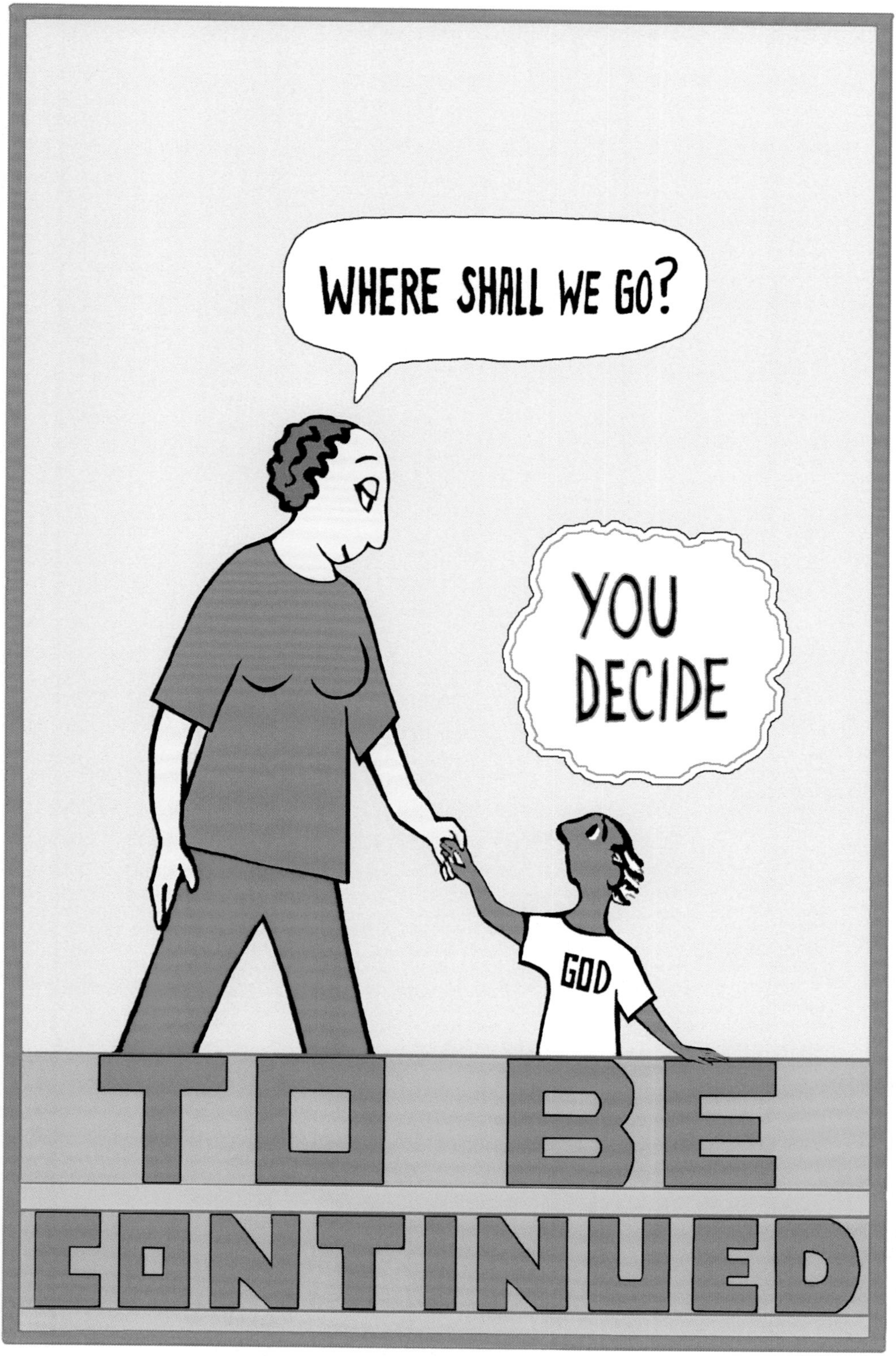
WHERE SHALL WE GO?
YOU DECIDE
GOD
TO BE CONTINUED

SOME COMMENTS BY VISITORS TO THE ONLINE VERSION POSTED IN 2004-2005 ON NATALIE d'ARBELOFF'S BLOG, *BLAUGUSTINE*.

I start to like Mr.God. He is more human than the God I know. I see that he shaved his beard prior to the interview and he looks younger than the God I met years ago. F.Sugar

The candid quality of this is what gives your conversations with God more impact.. There's something pure and truthful in stream of consciousness work. W.R.R.

I think you are subtly altering my mental image of God. I do the odd bit of praying and the T-shirted one seems to crop up quite often. Powerful stuff. Anna

Let's not complicate our lives by seeking, searching, thinking on "GOD" who for all actual, purposes is non-existant. Let's just be good humans and not good Christians or Muslims or Jews or Hindus etc. Sri

You've got a gentle way of making a point without being dogmatic. James

Now this is a God I might get along with..The only God with whom I'd want to share roomspace. Dick

But if you read those books God does most of all that other stuff! Crying, shouting, threatening, forgiving, vengeance. Walking out, not, we hope. (Sigh) Betty

But then Perfect Love begins to look like simple kindness. Is that what you mean? Or is there more to it? Dwight

It's wonderful: fresh, original, surprising, both poignant and funny. I love the "Now or Never" leaf and the way eternity dawns on the interviewer, if eternity can dawn? Beth

"That which cannot be imagined" is so dense with its power to compress a number of religions, Plato, and art! Maria

Your theology is almost persuasive! Perhaps that cul-de-sac I went down left me out of range for a signal. Red Baron

In the tradition of Job, Abraham at Mamre, Jacob wrestling with the "angel". Keep it up, this is great! Dave

I used to teach this kind of stuff (this I reckon is the "Irenean Theodicy"?) I tried to use some comic strips myself - wish your stuff had been around then. Psychbloke

I must be looking for God in all the wrong places. Thanks for putting up more signs. Kevin H.

This one really makes me think, Ouch! Ricon

Is that the Tree of the Knowledge of the Goods God Has on Everyone? Joel

This is the coolest thing I've seen in a LONG time. I hope it goes on....for eternity! Jackie

You managed to hit the nail on the head yet again. Absolutely brilliant! Cait

This series leaves me breathless.. Always amazed at the subtleties, the colours, the dry humour. When this lot gets published I'm buying everyone I know a copy. Coup de Vent

I like the dissonance of discussing such "high" topics in comic form. I didn't feel the usual intensity of theological discussion - I think the medium lessened the intensity without degrading the content at all. Beautiful work. Matt

Takin' a walk with God, how lovely! I'll be on the edge of my seat waiting to see how this one turns out. Lorianne

Obstinate Augustine reminds me of me... If there isn't ever another interview with the G-man, I'd still remain wowed. Excellent ...may you have a thousand page views. Elck

I just re-read through all the interviews....Ahh. They made me tear up - I could just feel the yearning in them. Do you believe in God? Sometimes I wish there was a God. April

You've made my day... it isn't you talking to God, it's me. Sheesh. Fran

From a Benedictine to an Augustinian - well done with your artwork, a real labour of love. The Gray Monk

I don't know how you do it but am glad every time you do - divine inspiration perhaps? Joe

Not being a believer anymore (sometimes I'm not sure I really was), you manage to capture the essence of a relationship with God that I find, er, realistic. Let me just say your conversations are inspired. Kathryn

I've been wrestling with this issue, myself. I'm thinking of throwing out my intellectual constructs about Meanings and Purposes. Wandering Willow

This is GREAT, GREAT stuff. I don't know how you knew what God looks like but I think you got it just right. Amba

Utterly wondrous! It's the way you manage to infallibly and simultaneously put a finger on both the deplorable zeitgeist and the divinely ineffable. Jean

I never get tired of God surprising Augustine. I think of God as not being a static being. I think of God's reality as being slippery and hard to capture in language..."Blessed are the poor in spirit. Theirs is the Kingdom of Heaven"....I think your picture of God has that quality. Real Live Preacher

Sometimes people want something firm, absolute and unquestionable.. What you..have given is a starting point from which the readers can begin to do their own work. Own work is good. This work is good. Gooder and gooder each time I look at it. Kim

I read it out loud and shared it with my kids. I figured if there was one lesson they could learn about God, this would be it. Sussura

I think the main meaning to interpret from all this is that you are a very gifted genius and we are all lucky. Demian

ABOUT THE AUTHOR

Natalie d'Arbeloff was born in Paris and lived in France, Paraguay, Brazil, the United States, Italy, Mexico and Canada before settling in London. She speaks those languages but thinks, writes and dreams mainly in English. Her visual languages are painting, printmaking, cartooning, and in recent years she has also been working with digital media. Her artists books, prints and paintings are in private and public collections internationally, including the National Art Library at the Victoria & Albert Museum, the Library of Congress and many other institutions. She is currently working on a graphic novel, an autobiography, her ever-expanding blog and, of course, further interviews with God.

website: *www.nataliedarbeloff.com*
blog: *www. nataliedarbeloff.com/ blaugustine.html*

Opposite page: Digital self-portrait. NdA 2006

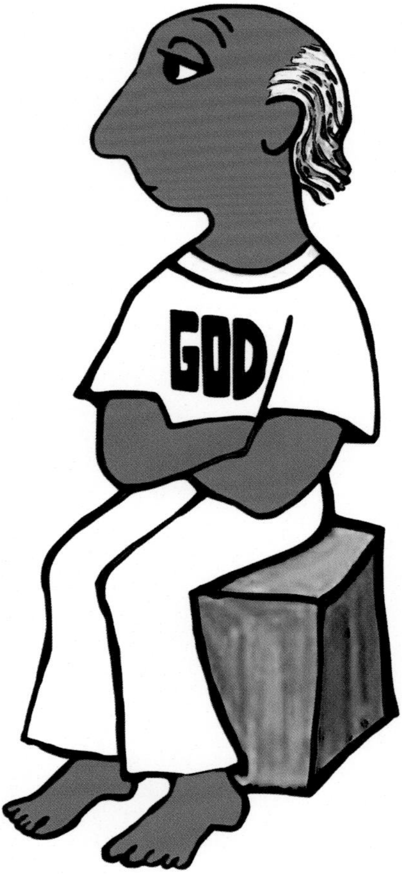
GOD